EDUCATION IN SEARCH OF THE SPIRIT

EDUCATION

IN SEARCH OF THE SPIRIT

Essays on American Education

JOHN F. GARDNER

✑ Anthroposophic Press

Previously published as *The Experience of Knowledge* by the Waldorf Press, Garden City, NY, 1975, this new edition has been revised, expanded and updated.

Copyright 1996 by John F. Gardner.

Published by Anthroposophic Press
RR 4 Box 94 A-1, Hudson, NY 12534

Library of Congress Cataloging-in-Publication Data

Gardner, John Fentress.
    Education in search of the spirit : essays on American education / John F. Gardner.
        p. cm.
    Rev., expanded, updated ed. of: The experience of knowledge. 1975.
    Includes bibliographical references
    ISBN 0-88010-439-2 (paper)
    1. Waldorf method of education—United States.   I. Gardner, John Fentress. Experience of Knowledge.   II. Title.
    LB1029.W34G37   1995   95-53215
                                                         CIP

10 9 8 7 6 5 4 3 2 1

Printed in the United States of America

Contents

Acknowledgments

To Harper & Row, Publishers, Inc. for permission to quote from Russell W. Davenport, *The Dignity of Man* (Copyright, 1955, by Institute for Creative Research, Inc.), and from Earl Kelley and Marie Rasey, *Education and the Nature of Man* (Copyright, 1952, by Harper & Brothers).

To the Viking Press, Inc. for permission to quote from Abraham H. Maslow, *The Farther Reaches of Human Nature* (Copyright, 1971, by Bertha G. Maslow).

To Kappa Delta Pi, An Honor Society in Education, P.O. Box A, West Lafayette, Indiana 47906, for permission to quote from Abraham H. Maslow, *Religions, Values, and Peak Experiences* (Copyright, 1964, by Kappa Delta Pi).

To D. Van Nostrand Company for permission to quote from Abraham H. Maslow, *Toward a Psychology of Being* (Copyright, 1962 and 1968, by Litton Publishing, Inc.).

To Alfred A. Knopf, Inc. for permission to quote from B. F. Skinner, *Beyond Freedom and Dignity* (Copyright, 1971, by B. F. Skinner).

To the Macmillan Company for permission to quote from B. F. Skinner, *Science and Human Behavior* (Copyright, 1953, by The Macmillan Company).

To the Rudolf Steiner Press for permission to quote from Rudolf Steiner, *The Philosophy of Freedom* (Copyright, 1964, by Rudolf Steiner Press).

To the U.S. Department of Health, Education, and Welfare for permission to quote from *Discovering Yourself in the Brain Age*.

To G. P. Putnam's Sons for permission to quote from John Dewey, *Education Today* (Copyright, 1940, by G. P. Putnam's Sons).

To *Education as an Art* for permission to quote John F. Gardner's article "Programmed Learning" (Vol. 28, No. 1 Summer, 1969).

To the Myrin Institute, Inc. for permission to reprint John F. Gardner's article "The Experience of Knowledge" *(Proceedings* No. 14, 1962) and from "Towards a Truly Public Education" *(Proceedings* No. 18, 1966). Both articles are copyrighted by the Myrin Institute in the years indicated.

Preface to 1975 Edition

THE FOLLOWING ESSAYS are drawn from three phases of my work during the last twenty-five years on the campus of Adelphi University, where I have served as faculty chairman of a nursery-through twelfth-grade school, the Waldorf School, and as director of a graduate program in teacher training, the Waldorf Institute for Liberal Education.

Part One arose from my earliest efforts to set in context the main problems, as I saw them, of modern education: namely, the need to bring thinking to life and the need for a spiritual concept of man.

Part Two contains the essay on teaching methods from which this book takes its title. It was written to acquaint parents with answers our Waldorf School was giving to the problems raised in Part One.

Part Three treats problems of special interest to parents and citizens. "Authority, Discipline and Freedom" attempts to clarify the mysterious way in which full-fledged freedom emerges for the maturing human being from his childish imitation of example, his youthful trust in and obedience to authority. "Genius as the Goal of Education" shows that, strange as it may seem, every child is close to genius, and that the primary goal of education should be to preserve and further enlist this genius. "The Next Step" addresses itself to the idea of cultural pluralism in a political democracy, its thesis being that if Western civilization is to begin resolving rather than compounding its difficulties, the present state school systems must make way for arrangements that will give much more freedom and responsibility to individual schools, providing parents at the same time with a correspondingly greater freedom of choice among schools. The Epilogue considers the implication of the foregoing arguments for America's leadership among nations.

The Appendices contain material that helps to set the rest of the book in context: they are meant less for scholarly reference than to be of interest to all who find themselves interested in the rest of the book.

J.F.G.

Foreword to the Second Edition

THE TITLE FOR THE FIRST EDITION of this book (*The Experience of Knowledge*) seemed significant at the time. Many leaders were then stressing the need to make education a genuine *experience*. They felt that when learning amounts only to the acquisition of knowledge, it becomes abstract, dry, deadening, and instinctively distasteful to healthy students. Hence they sought ways to bring the learning process to life, and to this end advanced the idea that learning should focus more upon an involvement in *doing*, so as to activate volitional as well as mental powers, thus enlisting students more fully in the pursuit of knowledge. To its credit, this impulse was driving toward education of the whole human being; it sought to replace death by life.

At that time, it had become clear to me, however, that much doing, when it alone is added to intellectual effort, does not yet provide the essential of what deserves to be called genuinely human experience —certainly not, if this doing becomes simply a matter of field trips, class projects, or even what too often pass for creative arts. These can all be very good, and they do tend to foster caring; but for *heart* to be touched more intimately and lastingly, and for real caring and commitment, something still more essential must be added to *mind* and *will*.

The riddle or problem of would-be holistic education comes into focus here. For what is it that truly touches the human heart, quickening it to "heartfelt" experience? Mere observations and thoughts do not suffice, even when action is added. For the deepest and yet freest kind of human concern, something else must allow the objects and events that are being perceived, thought about, and acted upon, to reveal aspects of themselves that are usually hidden. This something should be permitted and helped to reveal itself to the heart in intimate nearness. The title of this book's second edition has therefore been altered, further to emphasize just this often neglected, this hidden factor.

The kind of interaction serious educators are searching for, to take place between the soul of a student and all aspects of the world he or she is studying, must give precedence to the third center of human response that lies between the kind of knowing related to the brain and the kind of doing that stirs the abdomen, as it were, and activates the limbs. This third kind of power lives centrally, indeed, in the heart. We experience it most positively as love: love that is based upon wonder and trust, which grow and flourish in turn from the sense of deepened affinity to which education *should* lead. The joy-making, enlightening experience of affinity occurs, only when like, however, finds truly like —when the human soul draws near to soul and spirit realities beyond itself in the other beings, circumstances, and events it encounters in life.

Much has been written about soul in recent years by such subtle, caring observers as Thomas Moore and Robert Sardello. (Moore, *Care of the Soul*; Sardello, *Facing the World with Soul*). My own long-standing conviction—that creative realities of soul and spirit are to be discovered in or behind all things—I owe chiefly to the still more basic spiritual-scientific investigations of Rudolf Steiner. It was his insight into human nature in its relation to world nature that became a basis for the educational methods adopted by what are now widely known as "Waldorf" schools.

I believe strongly in the excellence and soundness of the new insights that stand behind the Waldorf impulse in education; but I am less than enthusiastic about accepting the name generally used to designate this impulse, for it gives no clue as to what the new beginning actually intends or involves. The first small school with its twelve teachers was established in Germany in 1919, chiefly for the children of workers in a "Waldorf-Astoria" factory. It meant to set an example of ways to renew wholesome humanity in the upcoming generation of an almost destroyed people. It prospered greatly and has led to the founding of some 600 other schools worldwide. But the name taken by the school obviously gave no hint at all of how it meant to achieve its goal. For this reason, I have come to wonder what kind of lead the "Waldorf" schools (*and* others that find themselves similarly motivated) might offer to inquirers, to give them at least some idea of what to expect. It has occurred to me that a subtitle such as the following might begin to suggest the simple but revolutionary ideal at work here:

SUCH-AND-SUCH WALDORF SCHOOL
A School of the Direct Approach

Considering the small likelihood of this subtitle being acclaimed, I offer it humorously even though seriously. The words convey little more than an impression, yet this impression does suggest certain qualities that should rightly characterize this kind of school. For one thing, it moves in a distinctly forward direction! "Direct" implies straightforward and honest, realistic and to the point. One may even feel the presence here of a certain courage to share values that are ordinarily wrapped in silence. Presumably one can expect such a school to note and mention and deal with subtle aspects of life in a plain, friendly, manner.

The "approach" in this subtitle suggests a definite will to face rather than to evade or flee from the "hidden" essential of whatever issue, person, or event confronts the teacher. Therewith the kinds of questions that make all the difference in education come to the fore: What factors are more essential than others in our efforts to understand, experience, and cope with life? Waldorf schools wish to come into touch with what is most basic not only in human nature, but in the nature of Nature itself, in the great universe within which we live.

How can this be done? Discussion leading to clear indications of method will of course be needed, especially if so-called Waldorf schools are to protect themselves from seeming to be the very opposite of what Rudolf Steiner meant them to be: namely, parochial enterprises seeking to advance a particular world-outlook, rather than to assure the unfolding of creative commitment and courage on the part of students, to achieve their own independent understanding and make their own free choices in a direct approach to the shaping of life.

The direct approach aims always to recognize and enlist the reality deeply hidden in the individual's own soul—what each truly admires, honors, hopes to discover more fully, and wants to become. It is this self that alone can sense and fathom the essential *being* within and behind all aspects of physical, earthly existence. This deeper self finds true affinity only with that hidden depth in others. The vital aspects—the soul and spiritual qualities—in Nature even as with one's fellow human beings, do not disclose themselves to the passing, or merely inquisitive, glance. Nor do they respond to anyone's desire to possess or use them. Their emergence awaits the ever-growing realization that follows simply from intensified wonder, delight, and grateful praise.

Direct approach is approach by one's own center of consciousness to the central identity of other beings. Only spirit finds spirit and knows it when it finds it: knowing how to look for it, how to test its reality, how to greet it, love it, and work with it within the grace of fruitful comradeship. Spirit calls unto spirit—draws it forth. As these approach and interpenetrate in the soul's experience, it comes to know security, peace, fulfill-ment, and new creative power. Harmony and goodness prevail —the veritable beginning of a new Heaven and a new Earth!

All the dissatisfactions and dissensions today, the anger and warfare, the loneliness and fear, the perverse pursuits of power and pleasure —not to mention the too sanguine hopes invested in such earnest initiatives as body-building, social planning, moral crusades, scientific discoveries, technical inventions, etc.—are but efforts to win fulfillment of the human soul's longing for peace and happiness. These become attainable, however, only when inquiry and commitment start from and engage the whole person. This process calls for the kind of ex-pectant trust that makes evident in reality that which otherwise remains unguessed and unseen.

The direct approach requires that one's quest for the spirit, the hidden essential in life, be made from the truly essential in one-self. Life puts to every human soul the question: "What do you *really* want?" Only the real Self can answer: "I truly want. . ." and really mean it—therewith to find itself directly, wholly, and har-moniously involved. Real education will always seek to strength-en what is best in the human soul: its longing for an experience of spiritual truth that brings to the fore an objective appreciation of the noble aspects of its own nature, together with a sense of real affinity with the rest of humanity, with the Earth planet as a whole, and with the great cosmos above and beyond us.

J.F.G.

Introduction

We Moderns are faced with the necessity of rediscovering the
life of the spirit; we must experience it anew for ourselves.
—C. G. Jung

THE ESSAYS in this book start from the premise that humanity
consists of beings of body, of soul, and of spirit. We are clearly
distinguished from the animals, who are also active and conscious, by the fact that our consciousness and activity can be
united in a single point that represents complete presence of
mind and at the same time, total will to action. As human beings, we refer to this fusion of wide-awake consciousness and active will into a single point when the word *I* is used. It is the basis
of our freedom to choose and to control our behavior. It is the
basis for moral responsibility and love. Our goal is to be fully
present in awareness and wholly in control of our behavior. We
may dream, as animals do, but we are not doomed to dream. Animal instincts may assert themselves in us; but we have at heart,
little by little, the ability to purge ourselves of merely instinctive
behavior. We would prefer at all times to know clearly what we
are doing, and we would prefer to do only what we ourselves intend according to clear knowledge that will please us permanently as well as momentarily. We would like our lives from moment
to moment to be known and authorized by that part of our being
which is forever.

In the core of our being, we are eternal spirit. Inevitably, we
strive to live from this spirit. Inevitably, the goal of the education
we give our children is to help them activate this deepest center
of being in themselves. We seek methods that show promise of
being able to awaken, draw forth, and strengthen what lies in our
children as the seed of all creativeness and joy in living.

But the spirit of human life on Earth does not stand naked. It is clothed in powers of soul and works through these powers. The human being thinks, feels, and wills. These forces are not equally developed from the beginning, and eventually they must be yoked together according to free choice, since of themselves they do not pull in a single direction. They contrast with and even contradict one another in their workings. One force—that of thinking—leads us beyond ourselves; it opens up the laws of the world around us. The polar opposite of thinking is volition. In exerting the force of will, we assert ourselves upon or against the world. Feeling mediates between thinking and will: it heralds the message that the world will awaken in the self, and it prepares the deed that the self will imprint upon the world.

The instability of the educational method in America during this century can be accounted for by the fact that now thinking, now feeling, and now will has been taken in turn as *the* clue to good education. But of course they must all be brought along. When any one is neglected, disturbances appear in the souls of the children being educated. When these disturbances become obvious enough to disturb the general public, they provoke the demand for a change in method. What are vaguely called "traditional" methods have usually emphasized the objective aspect of experience. They address themselves to memory and the power of thought, for these record and grasp what is going on in the world. What, with equal vagueness, have been known as "progressive" methods have tended, by contrast, to emphasize the subjective aspect of experience: impulse and feeling. They seek to bring forward the child's self, and ask children what *they* want to do, encouraging them to follow their own desires.

When formal academic learning has noticeably begun to put out the fire of enthusiasm in many students, it is only natural that some teachers should look for ways to rekindle it. And when the emotional or free "creative" approach has shown signs of fanning *subjective* flames out of control, it has been only prudent for teachers to box the children firmly in again and give them *objective* work to do. In both student and teacher, the one spirit that stands *behind* the several soul powers requires these shifts from knowing to feeling to doing, and back again. The human self is not free, cannot be in control, when education develops soul powers onesidedly. It is the very center of our humanity that requires and strives to establish in us the balance and harmony of functions. Integrity in either receiving or giving requires this condition of balance and poise in the soul.

Thus the dramatic reversals in education that have taken place every decade or so in this country, from the intellectual to the affective-active, and back again from the affective-active to the intellectual, are understandable. But they tend to extremes because they are a thrashing back and forth from one sick condition to the other. They are not healthy exchanges—as in normal breathing, which finds it good to breathe out and then equally good to breathe in—but repudiations and revolts.

Who or what can we believe is really to blame—that the accent upon academic learning should prove so depressing to the human spirit, and that the accent upon "emotional" response and "creativeness" becomes so egoistic? Does the appeal to objective reason necessarily cause atrophy of heart and will? Surely not, for sound, responsible thinking should obviously be willed through and through; it should also both use and renew the life of feeling. At the other pole, must creative activity banish mental discipline? One cannot suppose so, since the conscious act of creation surely requires a clear head. Why then should not the shifting emphasis in education, from the objective pole of learning to the subjective pole of will and feeling, and back again, be daily and gladly made to the profit of both sides, so that in every kind of school the emotionally charged, creative student becomes also a penetrating thinker; and the patient, disciplined student comes to be filled with an enthusiasm that will seek creative outlets?

Blame cannot be ascribed to the motives that have periodically brought about drastic reversals in the methods of education, since what moves teachers and parents, however obscurely, is always the wish to restore wholeness and balance in their children. Blame must go to certain ideas. These ideas have dominated schools for several generations. Though traditionalists and progressives may believe they are pursuing opposite goals, both usually take for granted, start from, and employ throughout, the same ideas. They work from very similar conceptions of human nature and the world in which we live. These concepts are adopted from the culture of our time. Our culture, in turn, utilizes the ideas developed by its scientists and philosophers of science.

Why do these particular "scientific" notions spell doom to the hope of awakening and strengthening the human spirit? The reason is that any education built upon them takes absolutely no account of the spirit, either in humanity or the world. Those who believe spirit to be purely hypothetical—and perhaps even an unnecessary hypothesis—are unable to build or support any bridge that could creatively lead the deepest powers of the human self creatively into the outside world, and bring the deepest enigmas of the outside world cognitively into the human self.

Strangely enough, the theory of knowledge on which modern science has based itself for several hundred years does not acknowledge that we *can* know the world. No doubt, we can find our way among things—we can put things to use—and on the basis of shrewdly formulated notions we can achieve some operational successes. But really get out of our own skin to *know* for sure, we cannot. We must be content to look on, and to guess and theorize; scientists today generally suppose that there is no way, no hope, of coming to know the deeper meaning of events. Contemporary science avoids both the light of ultimate meaning and the warmth of actual being, which are the very experiences the human heart wants from knowledge. It limits its inquiry to externals: physical substance and force.

Most simply stated, the present forms of natural science are able to investigate the world only insofar as the world is a mechanism. And in the final analysis the modern scientist tends to believe that the world—humanity itself, as well as the atoms and stars between which we hold an intermediate position—*is* a machine.

Perhaps only the physical sciences look for the machine in everything, including the human being, since psychology is mainly on the lookout for the animal in human nature. But educators who must draw from both kinds of science, are significantly influenced by both notions. Probably a majority of teachers at the present time, whether or not they have thought the matter through, pretty much take for granted that they are dealing with human animals within the context of a mechanistic world. Looking to the self, they see a biological organism; looking to the world, they see a cosmic mechanism. To the souls of children who long to knew what *human organism* and *world mechanism* essentially have to do with one another—beyond purely chance happenings or meaningless cause and effect sequences—they have nothing to say.

While the physical world conception of our time has helped us to establish our sense of being bodily individuals, and has looked after our physical welfare, it is certainly not capable of providing the inner light and warmth that nourish the human soul and spirit. It does not lastingly inspire or satisfy students in the one kind of school more than in the other. Traditional forms of education, working with the ideas given them by an agnostic, neutralized science, no longer lead the child on sure feet into God's world; rather, they are left at loose ends in the

emptiness of the "Great Meaningless Happening." And progressive educators are generally no more successful in their effort to discover and release the spiritual nature in the child,
since for most, scientific ideas have placed the animalistic
where one might have looked for the divine.

It happens, therefore, that while the objective emphasis in
education should fulfill students by opening them to the wonder of the world, too often the opposite takes place. Students
are bored, enervated, and depressed by what they learn. They
feel their humanity slipping away from them. Consequently,
many students either harden their hearts against their own humanity and decide to "make it" in the cold, hard world; or they
follow the beckoning of pseudo-idealism and are lead into the
diversions of alcohol, drugs, and eroticism. Perhaps some will
do both, while pursuing an ambition for power and status in
the world; they will also seek their fill of private pleasure. In
any case, the student who started in a school whose aim was *objectivity* feels, without changing schools, thoroughly imprisoned in *subjectivity*. Both in competitiveness and in self-
indulgence, the student becomes the very image of self-seeking
and self-concern.

It also happens that students who are exposed chiefly to the
subjective emphasis in education find themselves, in these same
schools, equally bored and depressed. Though their teachers
want them to feel encouraged to bring forth their own best in
an atmosphere of freedom, what these progressive students
glean of the great world outside themselves—in which they
would also like to be interested—is dull and disheartening. And
what they find when they look within themselves for the well-
springs of interest and creativeness is just instinct or whim. Students so educated feel their humanity suffocating. Though their
teachers may glorify sensitivity and caring, what they actually
bring forward as subject matter turns out to be not worth caring

deeply about. As for creativeness, little comes forth. The permissive nature of "free" schools hurts students most just where their teachers meant to build them up—specifically, in their self-esteem. Indulgence and easy praise never give young people the feeling of worth that comes from, on the one hand, a firm grounding in the realities of the outer world and, on the other hand, obedience to the higher judgment in each soul that wants to establish itself over against merely subjective impulses. It is not liberation of the animal within, but rather ascendancy of the higher self over the animal that gives a human being the autonomy and power of self-actualization.

The present conflict between the subjective and objective approaches to education is fruitless, even destructive, and cannot be made productive until these approaches are no longer in opposition to one another. We must learn to find that which is objective in the very heart of the subject, and that which is subjective in the very heart of the object. Only in this way can we convert a stalemate into a creative process.

So long as the essential energies of the self are imagined to be animal drives, and the essence of the world process is imagined as mechanistic, how can the human soul, which is innately and incorrigibly idealistic, feel at home? The soul will feel contempt for its own inner world, and remain a stranger in the surrounding world. What every human soul would really *like* is to find a loving, creative Selfhood somehow out there in the world, and a wise and noble Order here within itself. Then the individual could feel sure and capable within, and at home and beloved in the world. But while new educational methods have at last been developed that are capable of giving students this twofold healing experience, these methods require a spiritualized world conception. They call for a new theory of knowledge to support new insights into both world and self. To find God once again in both the human soul and the processes of nature requires a further evolution of thought-ability that can carry cognition beyond the ordinary limits of knowledge. As the following essays indicate, I believe the epistemology, the scientific method, of Rudolf Steiner[1] satisfies this requirement. It seems to me no accident that the founder of a spiritualized form of scientific inquiry should have been also the founder of the most thorough, most comprehensive answer to modern education's quest for renewal.

Steiner's methods of science and education are complex and difficult to master, but the way in which we can apply his general counsel about balanced human development to the present educational dilemma may be shortly summarized. To achieve an ardent, creative response to life without losing a firm hold on objective knowledge, skills, and discipline, a student needs to reverse the usual attitudes. According to Steiner, we must learn to be warm toward the world rather than warm about ourselves, and cool about ourselves rather than cool toward the world.

Let students be asked to take up facts and ideas about the natural world, the lore of science and history, with feeling as well as thinking. Let students pour creative power into observation of the world, identifying intimately with each thing observed—assessing, and reproducing as it were, these things within their own will. Let each form, color, and tone awaken within them a distinctive, active feeling; and let such feeling express itself through moral and artistic deeds.

Let the individual student learn to regard personal preferences, private needs, and desires, from a certain distance. Never let the student be "turned off" to the world, but rather to things that concern only the self. We do well to see ourselves as others see us, and to value our own affairs no more highly than others do. We should strive for objectivity above all concerning ourselves,

---

1. Austrian philosopher and educator, 1861–1925. See Appendix A.

since what is of greatest value is the element within us that determines, with absolute impartiality, the objective value of things. This is unbiased thought and the power of reason. In our inner life, desires should not dominate, but thinking should be foremost—especially the thinking directed toward *other* beings.

The thinking that results from this change in attitude will not be ordinary thinking—bloodless and abstract—but will begin with empathy and the involvement of soul. It will not seem at first to be thinking, but thinking will be the natural flowering of what it is. It will be feeling, but feeling that is disciplined and articulated by strict adherence to the qualities of existence that have awakened it. Feeling so directed will eventually coin itself into objective thought, and such deeply grounded thought will be all the more powerful, resonant, and creative for having been long in gestation.

Impersonal logic serves especially well when applied to personal feelings. And personal warmth never serves better than when it helps us to become intuitive concerning the facts and beings outside ourselves. We should be warm toward the world, however, not because it can supply our selfish needs but because in and of itself the world is beauty, wonder, and revelation. Contemplation of nature in the right way takes us out of ourselves, a thing for which we long; and self-forgetful love, in turn, fills our inner emptiness. To share cognitively and compassionately in the existing creation always charges the personal soul with new creative power.

There is a critical difference, with regard to the ultimate validity of human thought, between the usual scientific attitude and what is proposed here. This difference leads to divergent concepts of what method will best nurture thought through the various stages of its development from infancy to adulthood. Just this difference has everything to do with the dilemmas of modern education. We usually suppose that thinking is a subjective function. It happens *in* us, and therefore seems to be of our making. It appears to be something added by us to the events of the objective world. If this is true, it follows that a little thinking goes a long way, and more will go too far. It appears then that a sound procedure for a true knowledge of reality is to permit only an absolute minimum of "subjective" thinking, and to correct this as soon as possible by "objective" testing. We should restrict our thinking to the coolest, most formal generalizations, so that the least amount of bias will burden the results.

But such a procedure is based on a false premise. Thinking must in no way be considered "subjective." It is thinking alone that is capable of calling our attention in the first place to the distinction between subject and object. How can thinking belong only to the subject, when without thinking the subject could not *be cognized* as the subject, nor could the world *be cognized* as composed of objects? The distinction between subject and object is not only introduced by thinking; it is also overcome by thinking. Thinking takes place in and through the self, it is true; but its validity reaches beyond the self to the farthest world limits. When true thinking speaks inside the soul, it is the world itself that is speaking. The objects and events of the world utter their secrets in us; the thoughts we think—in so far as we let them develop life and character—*are* these secrets. But the secrets were already creative forces in the world before they came to be a comprehensible language in the soul.

If we hold this attitude toward the nature of thought, we shall begin to think quite differently from someone who uses thinking but does not trust it. Because we *do* trust, we will give ourselves to the work of objective thought with the greatest subjective enthusiasm and hope. We will pour into it our full energy, and ask not only the mind but the heart, breath, and limbs to join in the act of thinking. It will seem obvious to us that every soul power should be mobilized for cognition. In such thinking, our whole subjectivity is taken up into the act of thought—*and is thereby released from subjectivity*. The whole objective world, as it utters itself in this kind of thought, is released correspondingly from *objectivity*. When the soul of the knower has sacrificed subjective bias for the sake of pure knowledge of reality, that reality can in turn shed its mask of externality and reveal itself as living presence. When educators come to a right appreciation of the human capacity of intuitive thought, they will know how to build the bridge between self and world. They will see that the world can think itself in the human being. When it does so in the head alone, certain truths come to light; but they are not the truth that the heart or bowels of compassion need. There is no reason why the world, out of its deeper mysteries, cannot impart also to the heart what it craves, if only the heart will learn how to think.

The world can think itself in us to whatever depth we offer for the purpose. In this way only does the world complete itself. After higher powers have brought the world as far as its mute appearance, humanity, through fully awakened thinking, supplies the means by which these mute facts and events can advance to the stage of utterance. Only in the *human* soul can they reveal the inwardness of *their* nature, which is rooted, like our own, in the divine ground of being. By outward observation we know ourselves to be body, but through inward activity we prove to be soul and spirit. Similarly, insofar as we look on at nature from the outside, we confront only bodily processes; but through the whole-souled kind of thinking that love has transformed to intuitive vision, we can begin to discover personality and meaning in all phenomena. We are then on the way to finding God in the world; and it is this experience alone that has power to satisfy and empower, to summon and release, the divine creativeness in ourselves.

Educators who have confirmed for themselves this theory of knowledge will no longer have to oscillate and alternate between academic-traditional and affective-progressive methods. They can do full justice to both the human self and the world in every aspect of teaching, whether their initial accent is cognitive or creative.

PART ONE

1

The Loss of Spirit

The history of educational theory is marked by opposition
between the idea that education is development from within
and that it is formation from without. ——*John Dewey*

AMERICANS are active and intuitive people. This, and the fact
that traditional methods of education had worn thin to thread-
bareness, may have been what in the early part of this century
led to the new movement called *progressive education*. The progressives took issue with traditional educators primarily on the
problem of what intelligence—the ability to think successfully—is, and how this intelligence can best be developed. They
determined that twentieth century Americans could no longer
be satisfied with thinking trained in old-fashioned schools, by
methods derived from literary and religious traditions long outmoded by modern science. The progressives wanted schools to
be based on pragmatism. They aimed to educate an active, motivated intelligence that would cope with the practical realities
of the present time.

For more than fifty years, recurrent waves of educational reform here in America have opposed those who cling to tradition, because the reformers have felt that thinking should
occupy itself with *reality,* not with books—especially not with
old books. Thinking should arise from real-life situations. From
the beginning, it should be tuned to reality; in the end, it should

change reality. It should want, and be able at all times, to steer the course of practical events. Every child has a natural aptitude for such an active, forward-looking mentality, at least until academic formalism comes along to dishearten her or him.

It seems that the very spirit of America spoke in the early ideals of progressive education. It spoke against the weakness and sterility of an intellect ritualistically trained in academic skills. It spoke in favor of a living intelligence creatively immersed in the present flow of events. The new impulse said that such an intelligence, or power of thought, could help beleaguered humanity bear its burdens and solve its problems. But to develop this quality of thinking schools would have to radically change their ways.

Thus began the era of "activity" in the classroom—*learning by doing*—and a curriculum completely oriented by psychology. To insure enthusiasm, studies were pursued according to children's interest rather than according to logic. To insure practical application, studies were derived from "felt needs" and attempted to "solve problems." The question concerning which children's needs and problems were to give direction to any given day's work was settled by democratic vote instead of by the teacher's authority. Much of this emphasis upon interests, needs, and problems in the early, child-centered progressive school had the purpose of bringing motion, enthusiasm, and pertinence-to-life into the static formalities of the classroom. It also accounted for the unfastening of desks from floors, the allowing of children to walk about and speak freely, and the encouragement of projects, experiments, and field trips. The emergent "activity-curriculum" proposed to bring an end to passive listening—substituting spunky creativeness for meek remembering. It aimed to convert obedience to authority into the collaboration of peers, and to make study a task undertaken gladly because it served each child's here-and-now purposes rather than the irrelevant purposes of another people, place, or time. In short, the new "child-centered" methods tried to organize schooling so that the student should no longer have to postpone year after year the natural question, "What's in it for me?" To a marked degree, they brought the student's ego to the fore, supporting its present claims against all outside compulsions, especially those of the past.

Progressive education came upon the scene as a liberating force. In the name of freedom it championed the right of children to their "individual differences." It encouraged the expression of freedom in self-chosen activities and uncriticized creativeness. It expected freedom to flower when the hand of external authority— meaning that of teachers, parents, society, tradition—was lifted from young personalities, so that they could discover their own lively purposes. On the report card, if such were still used, progressive teachers abandoned the time-honored methods of evaluating achievement according to objective norms, in favor of painstaking comments on the child's attitude and effort. The commentary sometimes came even from the student. Since ego-building factors played such a large part in evaluation, failure or retention of students was rarely thought justified.

It must be acknowledged that these methods did indeed release initiative and bring zest into many schools. Some students began to regard school with an affection that had been notably lacking from the academic relationships of earlier eras. Yet progressive education never fully satisfied most people. Though some of its innovations were gradually adopted by all kinds of schools, there were other things about it that went against common sense. Children educated by these methods seemed in general too coarse and forward, and being unable either to accept adult discipline or to discipline themselves, they often lacked focus and tenacity. Their voices sometimes became too much heard. Adults often found them unduly given to passing judgment, without the knowledge or experience on which to build sound judgment. And their education appeared haphazard: advanced in some ways, primitive in others.

The pragmatism of progressive education tended also to ignore culture. It glorified raw energy at the expense of refinement. It took the objective discipline out of art. Although it set a premium on creativeness, art itself fell into insignificance. It became a private experience, mere "self-expression." Perhaps, for many progressively educated children, the subjective emphasis also undermined religion. Though religion might be treated with deference—because people have a right to their personal feelings—beneath such deference often lay the unconscious assumption that religious experience, as a product of the will to believe, has only subjective value. The attitudes fostered concerning both art and religion tended toward a sentimental affirmation that covered deeper disbelief. Even as many progressive educators spurned the idea of objective criteria in art, they had little understanding for curbs on freedom of action other than what might result from the pragmatic concern for overt consequences. The religious view that there exists in each individual something that is higher than the ordinary self, and that education should help this higher will to rule in life, was usually not part of the program.

The purely practical morality fostered by progressive attitudes lacked power also to control behavior when passion challenged conscience. Because progressive education tended to encourage the lower self at the expense of the higher, it probably also weakened the courage of many students to resist mass pressures. Progressive education, for all its pragmatism, did not in fact train young people to cope with the reality of the world they lived in, and ultimately, did not strengthen adequately a most important part of their individuality.

The flaw in progressive education can be seen in the fact that by making every effort to encourage the creative will in the individual child, it came to largely ignore the legitimate demands of the rest of the world. While it awakened enthusiasm, it often came up short on facts learned, on the systematic ordering of facts, and on certain social and intellectual skills needed to deal with facts.

With the turn of the political tide from New Deal liberalism to Eisenhower conservatism, education also turned back toward traditional forms. The cry went up for education in the old-fashioned way: plenty of organized subject matter, plenty of standardized tests, plenty of drill, and a crackdown on permissiveness. Parents wanted their children brought back to *reality*—meaning something outward-directed, something objective. This turn in education was accelerated by fierce competition arising from the pressures exerted on limited college facilities by an increasingly ambitious population. Other factors also contributed—above all, the humiliating decline of Western moral and technical prestige. The failure of morale among so many of our prisoners of war in Korea, the extraordinary increase of "juvenile delinquency," and the indolent arrogance of too many students sitting out their days in school, all seemed to imply that the personal, psychological approach to education had failed itself. Many parents felt that indulgent relativism would have to be replaced by something closer to the hardheaded absolutism of Soviet discipline, if we as a nation were to face the realities of the world situation.

For a considerable period after Russia launched the first space satellite in 1957, American education turned away from subjective goals and norms. It preferred to start from world facts, and to organize human resources to cope with those facts. It was no longer so solicitous about individual differences in ability nor so anxious to justify all students in their own eyes. The students were held to norms set by colleges and norms in turn set for the colleges by national military and economic policy. More mathematics, science, basic skills of communication were wanted, with a system to accommodate the tracking of several grades of ability. More competition and speed were sought—failure for the slow, and advanced placement for the fast.

A whole new generation of children steeled themselves under the lash of what we took to be reality. Though later, under Presidents Kennedy and Johnson, we showed some inclination again to abandon conservative social policies, in education the direction remained set toward the old-fashioned ideals of soaking up facts and rote learning of skills. We were still disposed to believe that technology, not psychology— objective, not subjective force—rules the world. Educators might have continued in this persuasion indefinitely, had they not been abruptly confronted by a resurgent wave of self-will that set the young against all established values, or values of "the establishment." The alienated 1960s counterculture made its appearance; youth became antirational and antisocial as never before. Some kept a footing in the speeded-up academic treadmill but periodically "freaked out" and "expanded" their minds in whatever way they could. Others simply dropped out of the race for objective goals in a conventional future, preferring to immerse themselves in deeply subjective experiences of the immediate present.

Basic education, the neo-traditional wave, simply had not worked. Its discipline had ignored the passions—and reaped the whirlwind. Dutiful students, because their feelings had not been used or fulfilled by the purely intellectual regimen, eventually exploded. They gave themselves over to the hedonism of sheer impulse. If formal studies had been without passion, passion was now without form.

We must remember that the real value of the traditional school inherited from Europe and the Middle Ages derived from the vitality of its distant past, which had been spiritually active, spiritually rich. It depended for its interest, its life, on these ties with a far past when religion was based on an actual experience of the spirit—a spirituality that long continued to provide some nourishment for humanistic studies and the liberal arts. We must recognize, however, that while this spirituality was real, the path to it is quite blocked now, and we cannot depend upon life still flowing adequately into education through a traditional religion. The school of earlier centuries had a strong bond with religious belief and practice, and this bond is effectively broken now. It also had a strong family-life behind it; families today are rarely able to do what they once did for the development of children. All this has changed, and with it, the mentality and living conditions of modern times, which means that by trying to go back to the "good old days" in education, the traditionalist is wishing for something that cannot be.

When we say today, "The children should learn subject matter," what we are actually asking is that they subject their humanity to the kind of dehumanized, technical knowledge now being handed down from colleges into secondary and elementary schools. In general, this knowledge does not come to us from the religion-saturated past at all; nor is it continuous with the older concept of humane studies. It is rather the product of a modern scientism that seeks a complete break with the "superstitions" of former ages. For the modern school child, "subject matter" means the popularized findings of modern science. This science today, in its popular form at least, is really a kind of spiritual wasteland. It's difficult for average people to get excited by a modern textbook on botany, zoology, optics, or acoustics, and the labs in many schools turn out to be the ugliest and dreariest rooms. While scientific studies excite a restless form of curiosity in some students, they awaken real wonder, which is the more spiritual quality, in few. We do say "Ah" and "Oh" about the size or distance of things, but that just about exhausts our psychic reaction to what is taught today. In the end, there is an undeniable tendency for the spiritual part of a child to turn aside in boredom. The moral inspiration of traditional studies scarcely exists any longer, and the human spirit really cannot find itself in modern scientism. Academic forms of education in our present age have become so emptily competitive that students can feel their inner life being squeezed out of them between heartless social pressures on the one hand, and equally heartless "scientific" objectivism on the other. But the most recent forms of progressive education, the "free" or "open" schools, despite their personal and social idealism, their subjective emphasis, still leave their students short of true self-confidence based in spiritual self-knowledge.

2

What Is Truly Human?

The waking have one and the same world; the sleeping turn aside everyone into a world of their own. —*Heraclitus*

PROGRESSIVISM has disappointed and continues to disappoint all hopes for a new spirit in education. This concept deals only with the parts of the human being that are asleep. Freeing the children's bodies and giving outlet to their needs and drives will not strengthen their waking spirit, if the teachers themselves have no real concept of the difference between the sleeping and waking human being.

Not only the liberals in education, but many of the conservatives as well, derive their idea of the human being from biological science, which continues to exert a dominant influence on modern psychology. Though the various persuasions in psychology vigorously differ among themselves, none has quite freed itself from the limiting conceptions of experimental, laboratory biology. This biology states that the human being is an organism, pure and simple. In the idea of the human being as no more than a biological organism we find the root of the failure of modern education to address the *real* child. B. F. Skinner has no more idea of the waking, self-existent spirit of a human being than has Freud or A. S. Neill. Even the concepts of self-actualization and self-transcendence developed by Abraham Maslow, and the humanistic "third force" in psychology, scrupulously avoid acknowledging the element in the human being that is independent of and potentially superior to genetic determination.[1]

---

1. See Appendix B for examples of "third force" psychology.

Years ago, when I first conceived the idea upon which this chapter is based, I was looking for a summary of the concept of human nature that was the basis for the progressive impulse of that time. I found a treasure-store of "organismic" ideas in a book widely used in the 1950s that, to my knowledge, has not in essentials been superseded.[2] It was an early version of the style of thinking that still dominates teacher education.[3] *Education and the Nature of Man* had the special advantage that it tried to draw educational conclusions directly from the broad spectrum of scientific findings it proposed to summarize. I could not believe that the healthy feeling of most parents and teachers would accept such a view of human nature, if they were clear about what was being presented; my indignation took the form of marginal questions and expostulations. These became so profuse that they had to be written separately. The result was the present chapter, which though its style differs somewhat from the rest of this book, may be helpful to those who like to follow a single, representative argument from beginning to end. The jacket blurb of *Education and the Nature of Man* says that it is "in effect a summary of the best modern scholarship on a science of man that takes account of the findings of anthropology, biology, physiology, psychology, psychiatry, and sociology." The text itself states:

> These facts are not now in the realm of opinion.... Each fact specified is as near truth as it is possible to come at the present time, and is based largely on laboratory evidence. (p. 15)

---

2. Earl Kelley and Marie Rasey, *Education and the Nature of Man* (New York, Harper & Brothers, 1952). Copyright, 1952, by Harper & Brothers.
3. More recent samples of psycho-biological conceptions of the nature of the human being, both clinical and lab-based, which differ only superficially from what Kelley and Rasey have to say about human capacities and values, will be found in Appendices B and C.

John Dewey wished this book well with the following statement:

> I have had only once in many recent years as much satisfy-
> ing intellectual agreement in reading the writings of others
> as I have had in reading this manuscript.

Over the greater part of this century, Dewey has been the philosopher of education who has most influenced American
schools, and from his statement of approval I believe we may
take it that these authors are trying to say in plain words what
Dewey meant to convey in his far more complex writings.

Let us turn, then, to the concept of human nature that is developed so authoritatively in *Education and the Nature of
Man.*

> We see, then, that the organism called man. . . (p.22)
> These characteristics . . . have to be taken into account
> when we plan to educate the organism. (p. 22)

We are being introduced to the concept that the human being
is a biological organism. This concept still supports most of
modern educational theory, and increasingly so. Schools are set
up to "educate" groupings of such organisms.

> Now, being an organism—what does that signify?
> . . . the human organism, being composed of atoms, is
> therefore an embodiment of energy, and energy is always
> seeking to spend itself as it can. (p. 23)

> We are coming to appreciate the fact that all matter is
> energy. We know from the structure of the atom that this
> is true. (p. 22)

The human organism is an accumulation of atoms, which is to say a purely material being. But we are asked to remind ourselves that all matter is energy. To be an energy-complex sounds more spirited than to be just an aggregate of atoms.

> We see the living organism, then, as a unit of energy seeking to spend itself. (p. 31)

This unit of energy will not soon run down, for it

> . . . possesses the capacity to convert energy in the form of food into energy in the form of organism, so that it can become larger or substitute new structure for old. (p. 31)

Does this organism sound like a human being—or like a vegetable? We should try to form the clearest possible picture of the organism that is here called a human being:

> What man really is, then, is a bulk of space, or an embodiment of energy. (p. 23)

If this is the concept educators have of what we *really* are, we wonder just what may be the nature of the honor they accord to this individual bulk of space or unit of energy. How can we account for the progressive emphasis, in the child-centered school, on the *individual* child and *individual* differences? Let us inquire into the question of what distinguishes one organism from another. We need to know this not only as parents or teachers but as citizens. Kelley and Rasey point out that

> The democratic ideal requires us to hold that all individuals have unique worth. . . . (p. 158)

The concept of the individual's uniqueness is not a startling one. Probably there is no one who would deny it. We can all of us see it all about us.... We know and accept the idea that this uniqueness is found throughout nature. (p. 42)

Even in the inorganic world, this uniqueness seems to exist. Crystals form, but there are no two of them alike. Nor would it be any easier to find two blades of grass in a field or two leaves in a forest that were exactly alike. (p. 43)

Individuality cannot be restricted to human beings, or even to biological organisms, since it is characteristic of even the inorganic world. It is simply a matter of difference. The individuality of one organism lies in its difference from another organism. When teachers look around in the classroom, they can see that some children are tall, some short; some are fat and some lean; some have brown hair and some blond. These are individual differences. But do these differences impart "unique worth?" We used to think that there was more to individuality than difference! Individuality was not something given but something that could with effort be achieved. There was no in-built assurance that people would carve paths that could distinguish them from their families, their time, and the mass of people who behave as twelve to the dozen. Some might accomplish this to some degree; none would achieve it wholly. But our authors would have it that everyone is a unique individuality, inevitably so, whether or not special initiative is summoned.

We must ask how any form of education that permits itself such views can possibly renew the spirit in education. Our criticism is not directed at these professors personally, since they are only trying to be exceptionally clear about certain ideas that they have gleaned, as they say, from laboratory science. Nor do we mock the thousands of good-hearted teachers who read texts of this kind so skimmingly and with such a bias of good will that they believe themselves engaged in a crusade to establish the unique worth of children, to liberate creative individuality, and so forth. Without doubt, these teachers are sincere. And because of their sincerity, they actually accomplish wonders that cannot be gainsaid and should not be belittled. But what is the real nature of this crusade, as so many leaders in the schools of education believe it to be?

The concept of biological individuality is clear enough. The idea is that each life starts with the egg and the sperm, which chance to meet. In the fertilized egg, the chromosomes and the genes are found in a distribution that is absolutely improbable of duplication. This combination is what we call the genetic uniqueness of the particular biological organism. And now we see this organism in an environment; and its environment is unique, too, if only because the organism is related to it spatially in a unique way. This biologically determined organism, interacting in its own eccentricity with its specific environment, is modified, and modifies the environment in turn; and this modification goes back and forth. And so we arrive at something more and more unique all the time. This is the explanation given by modern psychologists of all schools, as well as by Kelley and Rasey, for the fact that the biological organisms called human beings are individuals.

Obviously this conception ignores what philosophic and religious insights have always taught us, which is that the basis of individuality lies in the power of *self*-determination. Be it noted that none of us determines either our given genes or given environment. How then can we be morally responsible for how these two givens interact? If we are nothing but a complex interaction of the given genes plus, or times, the given environment, we shall never exist as *self*-determining individuals at all.

The second point to notice is that the kind of individuality our authors are setting before us is one wherein each of us differs from all other human beings. Such a concept of individuality has drastic consequences for social theory. One observes that the rather subjective, egoistic tendency of progressivism in education is usually matched by a strong drive toward social conformity, and we now begin to see one of the reasons why this is so. The social implications follow from the prevailing concept of individuality.

If our individuality consists in that which distinguishes or separates us from one another, then to hold society together we must suppress or expunge a good deal of this very individuality. We just can't permit *too* much individuality, if we want to hold together as a social group. Individuality can be tolerated in matters that are of no great social concern; but when social cohesion is at stake, we had better not trust it. To accent individual freedom in *important* questions would be to destroy society; for individuality is difference, and difference creates strife!

A much more basic concept of individuality, one with which we are familiar as coming to us from the past, particularly out of religious sources—a concept, however, that need not depend on the past or upon religious backgrounds but can be freshly intuited at any time—is this: Real individuality is something that *transcends* the separation between human beings. The reason we all seem to be so separated from one another is that in each of us a spark of the one divine fire has individualized itself by descending into a particular environment, and clothing itself with a particular genetic structure. When these external elements manage to conceal the one fire[4] to be found in each of us, they make us seem wholly separate beings. It is the bodily

---

4. "It is one central fire, which, flaming now out of the lips of Etna, lightens the capes of Sicily, and now out of the throat of Vesuvius, illuminates the towers and vineyards of Naples. It is one light which beams out of a thousand stars. It is one soul which animates all men."
—R. W. Emerson, *The American Scholar*

structure and the environmental conditioning that intervene
between individual human beings. But the body thus specialized is not our individuality. We feel ourselves to be *in* this
body but not essentially *of* it. Ultimately, the material body
proves to be just as environmental to the real self as do its wider
physical surroundings.

Our real individuality is just what unites us with others. For
example, when scientists begin to think intensively, devotedly,
painfully, in solitude, about a matter of real inner concern—
when, in other words, being the real scientist they most of all
want to be—it is they themselves who are active. Their individualities push to one side personal predilections and eccentricities,
together with thought habits that have come from tradition or
training. And as this deeper individuality comes to the fore, what
it finds and gives to such scientists is of universal significance. It
expresses permanent, objective laws, and it has lasting significance for others who can think. Similarly, when poets or artists
bring substance forth from the solitary depths of their true individualities, what is offered will give immediate as well as lasting
nourishment to all people. The depths of the individual in each
case is spiritual, and the signature of the spirit is universality.

But let us go on to find out more about the nature of humanity as conceptualized, according to Kelley and Rasey, by most
biologists and psychologists. One of the basic things important
for any concept of morally responsible selfhood is the idea of the
human will. It is of crucial importance to know what scientists
think about the concept of humanity's power to set out and ex-
ecute self-initiated purposes.

What we mean by the term "purpose" is a driving force
which gives expression for, or points a path to, the expen-
diture of the energy of which we consist. (p. 56)

The driving force thus conceived is mostly a subconscious thing. We may have our conscious purposes, but conscious purpose is "less well established, more tentative, and more in need of validation." (p. 57)

Conscious purpose may be modified within limits. The limits are that no activity which violates the deeper unconscious purposes of the organism can become a true conscious purpose. (p. 57)

This is to say that we may, if we wish, choose certain purposes consciously—so long as these purposes do not interfere with our real purposes. These latter lie within the biological organism. Consciousness may not contravene them. The unconscious purposes are the true, sound purposes. Conscious purposes are flickering; and they may work against life. The genuine purposes of a human being, the things that actually do, and should, determine his behavior, are the deeper, unconscious purposes.

The unconscious purpose may be called tissue purpose, since there is evidence of its existence in all living tissue.... (p. 57)

The term *unconscious purpose* would seem to normal thinking a self-contradiction, since if I do not *know* my purpose, how can it be called mine? Sigmund Freud, however, has accustomed us to the idea that beneath our conscious intention, working with it or against it, often lies something deeply rooted in instinctual drives. Perhaps this is what is meant by *tissue purpose.*

Tissue purpose operates in a human being much the same as in a tomato plant. (p. 57)

The driving force of tissue purpose. . . points the way by which the good life for any unique individual may be lived. It is the force through which the plant, the animal, and the human being becomes more perfectly that which it already is. (p. 61)[5]

Here we come to a memorable statement. A child's purpose is to become more and more what, biologically speaking, she or he already is. Yet if there is anything characteristic of a human being it is that we are continually overcoming what we already are; and to the very extent that we transform our organic structure, our environment, and all the other things that "already are," to that extent do we consider ourselves worthy human beings. Such a view stands in opposition to what Kelley and Rasey have proposed.

I once heard a well-known progressive educator from a large university say, "We used to think that education taught children how to climb a ladder—how to make an arduous moral ascent. This was the idea of education we tried to inculcate into them. But now we know better. Now we know that life is easy, learning is easy—just like going down a chute!" Kelley and Rasey have expressed the alleged scientific basis for this view of human development. Human nature is seen by them as a something given, not achieved.

---

5. Maslow, in *The Farther Reaches of Human Nature*, pp. 186-7, supports this same idea: "Discovering your species-hoods at a deep enough level, merges with discovering your selfhood Becoming (learning how to be) fully human means learning (subjectively experiencing) what you peculiarly are, how you are you, what your potentialities are, what your style is, what your pace is, what your tastes are, what your values are, what direction your body is going, where your personal biology is taking you, i.e., how you are *different* from others And at the same time it means to be a human animal like other human animals, i.e., how you are *similar* to others."

For more on Maslow's concept of ethical purpose and value, see Appendix B, Part 2.

There seems to be a good deal of evidence that purpose is provided for in the genes.... These genes are the building blocks and building plan. As the sperm and egg are infinitely unique, so, then, is the purpose. (p. 58)

It may be that the philosophers who labored over the will, who made *will* a noun, and set it up as a faculty of the mind, were really concerned with tissue purpose... (p.57)

In reply, we must ask again: Is *tissue purpose* morally responsible?

Having now gained the idea of will as *tissue purpose*, let us go on to ask about the other capacity that is so very important in education, the capacity to know. This is really central, since children go to school primarily in order to increase their knowledge and their ability to know.

A great many of these living organisms have the power or capacity to know ... (p. 31)

The organism knows something it did not know before .... (p. 37)

It is simply what the organism knows. (p. 37)

Can we admit that the *organism* knows, when *we* know that as students we sometimes had, as it were, to beat the organism to keep it awake so that *we* could learn the things *we* wanted to learn?

... the nervous system has developed ways of interpreting [stimuli] ... (p. 32)

Common sense can readily accept that the nervous system transmits, but does it really interpret? To say so, as biologists commonly do, is to maintain as well that in perception it is not a person who sees through eyes, but eyes themselves that do the seeing. It is ears that hear: not a person who is hearing by means of ears.

This idea that the organism perceives and knows is not something to be laughed off. It appears to be the view almost universally accepted by educational psychologists, who differ more on other subjects.[6] Somehow it doesn't strike psychologists as ridiculous to say that the eye sees and the ear hears. They do not in the least share William Blake's view:

> This life's dim windows of the soul
> Distort the heavens from pole to pole
> And lead you to believe a lie
> When you see with not through the eye.

But one would like to raise a question: If it were so that the eye did the seeing and the ear did the hearing, what would join all these dissimilar perceptions together into unitary knowledge? How would there ever be the slightest interrelationship between the eye that saw and the ear that heard? Surely we can understand the unitary consciousness that combines all sense-impressions only by understanding that it is we ourselves—not our brains of many parts and millions of neurons, but we ourselves in our indivisible integrity—who see through the eye, who hear through the ear, and who think with the brain. Surely it is essential for educators, above all, to realize that knowing can never be organic. Cognition is actually and always *anti*-organic, for if knowledge of that which is *not* the organism is to enter, the organism itself must somehow give way.

---

6. See Appendix C, Part I, giving excerpts from a pamphlet widely distributed by the U S. Department of Health, Education and Welfare in 1974.

We have arrived at the basic element in any theory of education: the concept of knowledge. For the scientists honored by Kelley and Rasey, knowledge is a kind of activity of the organism. Let us follow this thought, to see where it leads.

The organism, our authors say, can grab things, it can move around, it can eat. The organism can digest, it can propagate—and it can think. Thinking is one of the things the human organism can do. Thinking is an *organic* activity. And because we are unique organically, our thinking, too, is going to be unique. Obviously the thinking of each of us, being the function of a unique organism, will therefore be peculiar to each individual.

We see at once how deep the opposition is between this still current view and what old-fashioned parents and teachers had in mind when they insisted upon knowledge of subject matter—when they implored "Let the kids learn facts!" For some educational psychologists and philosophers, these objective facts simply evaporate. It isn't just pigheadedness that makes such educators not worry too much about facts; it is the deeply felt conviction that these objective facts don't really, in the final analysis, exist.

> The view of many philosophers and educators makes knowledge something which exists in its own right, and portrays the organism as acquiring it much as the amoeba flows around food. This concept holds knowledge to be the same no matter who acquires it. (p. 37)

One might wager that many parents and teachers still have this very idea, but now they are asked to recognize and admit the completely subjective nature of cognitive life. Because each of us is an individual organism, each is unique; and because it is the unique organism that knows, the knowledge itself that each of us arrives at is also *sui generis*.

What is real in any situation is not the object that started the sequence, for it can be many things to as many men, but the individual interpretation put upon it . . . the object itself will always remain what an individual makes it as he interprets the stimuli brought to him by his receptors. (p. 33)

All our perceptions come from us, not from our externality . . . (p. 33)

One of the topical headings in this book is "What We Know Comes From Us."

Knowledge, then, is what we know. . . . It is subjective in nature, and unique to the learner. It does not exist before learning begins; or if it does, that fact does not matter. It is a result of process, and is subject to continuous modification. (p. 38)

When the organism changes, its knowing and what it knows will change, too. Knowledge changes from time to time, from person to person, and from me today to me tomorrow. There is nothing stable there in itself.

Cognitive life is thus seen to be almost entirely subjective. (p. 33)

Now we come to the conclusion:

Since perception and experience are subjective and personal, the residual knowledge also is subjective and personal. This fact gives each man a world all his own. (p. 41)

That each person sees only a private universe has social implications, for it

> . . . makes his problem one of establishing communication with others living in unique worlds, to the end that sufficient understanding will result that life will be tenable. (p. 41)

A somber note—at bottom, the writers are depressed, and understandably so; this doctrine is disheartening. Each of us is thus the "man in the iron mask." We are each doomed by our own organisms to solitary confinement for life. There is an insurmountable barrier that separates human beings from knowledge of each other.

> . . . what man perceives, what he knows, what he becomes is strictly his own and no other's. . . . Therefore we come to the inescapable fact that we have no given common world with our fellow men. Each sees his own world, and makes his own interpretations, and the differences in our seeing build us differently. (pp. 38-39)

> Some people, when they encounter the idea that we have no given common world, consider that fact extremely discouraging and productive of pessimism. They say that if this is true, then we have no basis on which to operate, no place to begin, and that the human race is therefore doomed to misunderstanding, strife, and war. (p. 39)

The authors are certainly right in saying that such a view of human cognition could give rise to pessimism concerning the possibilities of peace on Earth among humankind. This is the end to which this argument inescapably leads—unless, like these particular educators and others whose premises bring them to these same conclusions, one simply jumps the tracks of logic and makes an escape into wishful thinking. Kelley and Rasey escape the horrible prison of the subjectivist theory of knowledge by the simple expedient of being inconsistent with their own idea. Having just stated that knowledge is subjective, they go on to make it objective, as by saying, "After all, we all live on the same Earth"—as though in this "fact" we can find at least some basis for community. But one person must ask the other, "If *your* perception, understanding, and interpretation of this Earth we live on, and *my* perception, understanding, and interpretation of it are uniquely separate, how do we know at all that we live on the same Earth?"

The sheer impracticality of such subjectivism is striking. What about its moral implications?

> Because of the uniqueness of individual purpose, the individual views whatever he takes in from the standpoint of his own enhancement and defense.... Since this purpose to enhance or defend is ever present and automatic, we automatically place value judgments on what we perceive. (pp. 73-4)

> As the organism makes its way through life it is primarily concerned with its own enhancement and defense. (p. 126)

> The organism has its own ego to enhance and to defend. (p. 92)

We note that not the ego has its own organism, but the organism has its own ego! The drives attributed to the tissues of the human organism seem to be absolutely egoistic: we are not only limited to our own viewpoints; we also *care* only about ourselves. The authors admit that society becomes an outright impossibility under these conditions, unless we can now attribute to organic tissue a saving grace. The new quality upon which they rely to snatch us back from pure savagery is a second *tissue purpose*. We are told that beside the drive to enhance and defend ourselves individually, we have another tissue-urge that drives us to want other people. We need others; we have an organic need to be social.

Man needs freedom and he also needs other people. (p. 103)

The organism's social demands require . . . (p. 91)

This reaching out towards others is the natural effort of the organism to overcome its seclusion. (p. 39)

The powerful need each has for others, if given any kind of chance at all, would drive them together for the satisfaction of mutual social hunger. (p. 92)

Competition is untenable because it . . . deprives the individual organism of his full equipment of satisfied social need. (p. 94)

It may seem that to unite with other human beings freely, with interest and love, is a far cry from being driven to labor and mingle with them blindly, for the "satisfaction of mutual social hunger." However, for the view we are considering, social hunger needs only the addition of some canny reckoning in order to establish itself as a dynamic formula for altruism.

But before we follow this thought to the end, we should pause as our authors do, to comment upon the fact that we have here an excellent illustration of how some educators attempt to reconcile what they think of as science with what they understand to be the moral and spiritual teachings of our religious heritage. In *Education and the Nature of Man* we are told that:

> The old conflict between science and religion no longer needs to persist. From the beginning it should have been clear to us that science and religion could not be in basic conflict. What we are now learning from science . . . reveals the verity of the teachings we have had from great religious leaders. . . . (p. 159)

> Were there time and space, it would be interesting to take a large number of the great religious teachings and reinterpret them in relation to the unifying principle of man and his environment, or to the transaction of living. It would reveal the necessity of doing unto others as we would that they do unto us; why it is that as ye do it unto the least of these ye do it unto me. (p. 160)

Who can deny that the reconciliation of scientific thinking with moral and spiritual intuitions is sorely needed in the modern world? Kelley and Rasey say that a progressive psychology of education can show us how to achieve this goal in such a case as the conflict between the organic drive to self-enhancement and the spiritual ideal of altruism, or selfless love. Let us see whether what follows is dynamic altruism—or a kind of moral cannibalism.

> Others thus become as essential as food or shelter. Since others are essential, no man can be unmindful of others. Being mindful of others, seeing that others survive to fulfill one's social need, is the essence of cooperation. (p. 30)

Because of the relationship between us as human beings and our environment, where each builds the other, we can end our confusion about what is selfish. Enlightened self-interest and selflessness become the same. When the individual acts in full realization of his own need of others, he enhances the other in his own behalf. (p. 158)

Our own quality, then, depends upon the quality of the people out of whom we are built. Thus, we can see that adequate, decent human relations become not just something which is nice to have but a necessity for our own development. If we do not have people of quality around us, we will not have good stuff for our own growth. (p. 157)

. . . other people are what we feed on. . . . (p. 162)

Since I am built out of the quality of my brother, and since I cannot be better than the stuff of which I am built, I had better be my brother's keeper, cherishing him as I cherish myself. (p. 160)

For those whose common sense has not deserted them, this line of reasoning hardly needs comment. Christ said, "Whoever seeketh his life shall lose it, but whoever loseth life for my sake shall gain it." That is the religious teaching; but is it not the same as, "When the individual acts in full realization of the need for others, the other is enhanced in one's own behalf?"

As we saw in the relation of *thinking* to the organism, organicists do not permit themselves to visualize the difficult truth of *moral* behavior—that in morally responsible actions a higher principle enters and suppresses the lower. Even as every act of willed thinking suppresses organic life, so in altruism a greater, freer self permeates and transmutes the biologically limited self.

This higher (or deeper) self—the spiritual being in a human being—does not identify itself more with this body of mine than with that body of my neighbor. It cannot accept the point of view of any single body. It acts not in full realization of its own need for others, but self-forgetfully, in full realization of the varied needs of those others. Its fulfillment comes from enhancing the other for the very sake of the other. It does not consume others for self-nourishment, but in the enactment of the will to conscious responsibility, gladly consumes its own body, to generate spiritual warmth and light for others.

While it is true that there is an analogy to be found between organic behavior and spiritual life, we must realize that analogy does not mean identity. To travel from east to west is analogous to traveling from west to east, only the travel is in opposite directions. The embrace of battle may closely resemble the embrace of love, and the sacrifice of a lesser for a greater bears a strong resemblance to the sacrifice of a greater for a lesser. These are all partly valid analogies, but how disastrous to confuse the one with the other!

Kelley and Rasey, along with many educators who imagine that science supports their philosophic bias, reject the idea of self-transcendence as being dualistic. But one must reply, "If self-transcendence appears to be dualism—let us make the most of it!" Let us not be frightened by dualistic appearance; true unities are often made of such. For it is neither puritanical nor other-worldly, but simply practical and obvious to state that the nature of human nature, in many basic ways, is to counter nature, and that the way to human fulfillment is: "Die as organism, to become as human being!"

3

More Than Organism

In the idea is the true communion of human beings.
— Rudolf Steiner

IN THE PRECEDING CHAPTER we began to see how ill-starred any methods of education will be when they base themselves upon an organic concept of the human being, with no idea of the self-transcending, organism-cancelling work of universal reason in humanity. Such methods may pretend to release the ego of the child, but they actually blind and imprison. They make a child the slave of an instinctive, all-compelling selfishness. If the premise that human beings are simply organisms were true, children could never awaken to the light of *common* day. They could not know themselves, nor could they know one another. These things become possible only for one who finds in the organism an element at work that rises above and free from it: the power of reason.

If the notion that human beings are essentially, ultimately, no more than biological organisms destroys objective knowledge, what does it do to the subjective will and feelings?

If we as human beings can never get outside our own tissue far enough to know another being, we can never feel love; for love requires self-forgetful experience of the other. But both knowledge and love are essential to the functioning of the human will. Lacking the guidance of clear knowing and the motive power of love, human purpose sinks into moral inertia— or, led on by bodily appetites, wanders into byways. Without the fully conscious mastery of ourselves and the world, we must fall back upon the instincts that guide animals in their half-consciousness. But where the animal has vivid, unquestionable instincts, the human being has a near vacuum that is *meant* to be filled by world-encompassing intelligence. Failing to kindle the light of reason within ourselves, we remain essentially helpless—an impoverished, pitiable species of animal.

It is easy to reduce the idea of "human being as bodily organism" to absurdity on all counts, yet it is the prevailing idea today in educational psychology. It undermines every possible ideal about what education can do for children. Traditional and progressive ideals are both doomed. The former ideals place emphasis upon the "light of learning" rather than feeling, but how can mere organisms ever be brought to *see* this light? Actually, though the fact is little noticed, much of academic training today has nothing to do with seeing *light*. Not "understanding" in the true, free sense of the word but "performance" is now the goal. Organisms cannot really understand, but they can be trained to perform. Memory circuits can be imprinted in them. Conditioned behavior can be elicited from them.[1] If the mechanical computer and robot can achieve a high measure of efficiency, why not biological organisms?

Efficient habits are the goal of methods that stand in the direct line of descent from traditional education but have lost confidence in the organism-transcending power of reason. This efficiency is not a matter of inner light dawning, but of programmed behavior emerging according to schedule.[2] The model for the human being is the machine—human organisms are to be "raised" to the level of reliability attained by the best machines. In some particulars, we even hope to go beyond machines; but machines will teach, and test us.

---

1. See Appendix D, Part 1.
2. See Appendix D, Part 2.

In many states, recent laws have made "performance-based" teacher education and teacher certification mandatory. These laws are doubtless the work of conservative or traditional thinking. They are enacted by those weary of subjectivism, weary of enthusiasm, promises, and excuses. Such call upon education to stand forth from the morass of its vague imaginings and be tested by objective results. Yet laudable as the new call for accountability may be, one sees with sorrow and dread what is becoming of it in a day that cannot rise above the materialistic concept of humanity. For those pressing to make teachers "accountable," results do not mean objective spiritual values like compassion, generosity, and courage—to say nothing of integrity, idealism, or creativeness. Such values were the goals of traditional education when it was still religious; but for neo-traditionalists, ideals such as these are simply words; and words are wind, except as they move bodies. Let us see the bodies move! Let us have explicit, overt *performance.* Of interior states of warmth, illumination, fecundity, and grace in the alleged human soul we know nothing. Nor do we believe there is any responsible way to know.[3] But we do perceive when bodies move. Let us aim at that!

What is the root of the prevalent doubt that trained insight can perfectly well look into the inner life and see what grows, develops, and perfects itself there? Is it not the line of thinking that goes back through all varieties of biology, psychology, anthropology, and sociology that build upon the idea of the human being as a merely biological entity? This kind of thinking prides itself on having risen to the idea that we are more than mechanisms: behold, we are biological organisms! Such organisms live by habit, and habits can be trained: education should get on with the business of habit-formation. Society needs

---

3. See Appendix C, Part 2.

myriad organisms of proven ability to calculate, store facts, manipulate symbols, and manage situations.[4]

Before state laws based upon biological concepts of human nature had gone so far as to abolish the inward life altogether by giving attention exclusively to overt performance, education had passed through a phase that already showed which way the tide was running. Old-fashioned teachers used to speak of "understanding," "insight," and "appreciation." By such terms they meant to indicate that realm of inner experience whose perfect unity, whose radiant self-identity gives light and warmth to any fact or concept brought within it. *Understanding* occurred when what had stood outside in darkness was able to enter and become part of this one universal light. There was only one light, because it was inconceivable that *intelligibility* could be other than one. To say "I see," "I understand," meant that for me a given fact or idea had membered itself at last within the one world of reason. But organismic notions, following

---

4. "Factors of two kinds, according to Dewey, constitute the nature of every human being—force and pattern. Force (Dewey calls it 'impulse') is the fluorescence of living tissue; and as a consequence of it, the human being is constantly active. There is no direction immanent in this activity; the behavior of the infant is random and aimless. But very quickly, a pattern is assumed by impulse; and in that pattern, impulse finds a direction and a goal. This impulse is innate to the human creature, but the pattern in which impulse is manifested (Dewey calls it 'habit') is entirely acquired.

"Dewey tries to show that knowing is a kind of action; and to do so he makes use of his theory of human nature. Impulse must find a goal, and it finds it in habit. The organism whose impulse is thus channeled is adjusted. Still, habit sometimes breaks down. Intelligence is a way in which adjustment is re-established in these circumstances.

"Solving a problem amounts to acting upon the environment in order to bring about some consequence—to a rearrangement of our habits so that impulse can achieve its goal of smooth release.... Intelligence is the habit of responding in this way to problematic situations."—Kingsley Price, *Education and Philosophical Thought,* pp. 462, 469, 470.

in the steps of earlier reasons for philosophic skepticism, caused the inner light that lights everyone alike to grow so dim for most educators that it was quite darkened by what stands so very plainly before us in the *outer* light—the multitude of separate material bodies. The essence of materialism is a bias toward externality, and an external way of observing tends to lose itself in *things*, in the many. The bias of materialism favors multiplicity over unity. It feels sure about the many, since these are perceived by the physical senses; but it feels unsure of any unity, since an indivisible unity can be grasped only intuitively, by active thinking. Of thinking, materialism is always ultimately skeptical.

And so we came historically to the *plural* of these important words, which had hitherto always been singular. Materialism tore reason apart into reasons. Though obviously some portion of what used to be called understanding, insight, or appreciation, in the singular, was still lighting up from time to time in individuals (else all culture and social intercourse would in fact have ceased), educational theorists were no longer able to perceive how it is that while a particular individual may make many distinct *efforts* to understand, actual understanding takes place only when, and to the extent that, what had been apparently separated in external existence finds its place at last in the seamless light of inner realization. Nor could materialistically inclined educators appreciate how indispensable for the conduct of all aspects of human life is this unity that extends beyond the particular person to embrace others—as well as everything above, below, or around humankind.

To pluralize understanding is to divide every person from every other, not temporarily but permanently. It makes an idiot of each individual within the whole of humanity, and then it splits individuals within themselves.

Although, as mentioned, good-hearted, well-meaning, and altogether necessary motives lie behind the contrasting efforts of both the traditional academic and the newer affective movements in education, the organismic concept of human nature is incapable of solving the problem that holds them apart—specifically, the problem of how to relate subjective with objective experience. The drastic inadequacy of this seemingly innocent concept of "human being as organism" is what prevents us today from developing an educational method fit for human beings. Before we can arrive at a true understanding of human nature, we shall have to see through this idea—and see through, as well, the limitations of the kind of laboratory science from which it comes. Scientific method itself must dig to deeper foundations. These foundations will not be found, however, until scientists see the possibility and the necessity to develop thinking beyond its present weakness and self-doubt—to bring it to life as the climax of humanity's whole capacity for experience. Active, love-filled thinking is worthy of our trust. It waits, educational method waits with it, and the whole of modern culture as it issues from education waits, for the further development of thinking, based on such well-deserved trust. It is intuitive thought alone that can, in a single act, plumb the depths of objective reality and at the same time satisfy the innermost needs of the human soul for understanding and for love.[5]

---

5. See Appendix E, Part 1.

4

Thinking Brought to Life

Thought is a man in his wholeness, wholly attending.
—D. H. Lawrence

WE MUST GET TO THE BOTTOM of what makes studies so often dreary for children. That is the root problem for modern education. How do you bring children and their studies together, so that education becomes a spirited affair, and children grow spiritually? This chasm between a modern child and the studies prescribed is the same abyss that yawns between the souls of countless modern men and women, and the practical duties of the world in which they find themselves.

The reason for the split between the subjective longings of the human soul and the objective demands of life in the world is the fact that we do not trust, and so do not develop through education, the single bond that can truly unite the two. This one bond that can in freedom, consciously, lovingly, creatively unite humanity and world, child and studies, subject and object, is to be looked for in the active life of thought. It is neither biological instinct, as the progressives suppose, nor social conditioning, as the most modern traditionalists, the behaviorists, propose, that can do this deed. It is fully developed thinking.

Our lack of confidence in thought began at the time when modern experimentalism arose. One cannot say this shouldn't have happened; it was obviously required by human evolution. But when we began to depend so much on physical experimentation as to believe it the *only* method of scientific proof, it was clear that we no longer believed in the power of thought to guide itself, judge itself, correct itself: in other words, to find truth. We then had to steer our thinking from outside, verify it from outside, give it content from outside. Though there was once a time when people would take alleged facts and test them against the trusted power of the complete experience called thought, the self-limitation of thinking to purely abstract operations has brought us to the point where now we must try any and all thoughts by the only evidence we now trust, which is that of the physical senses.

We have lost our trust in thought because our manner of thought has changed until we can no longer believe that reality could possibly express itself through such thinking. Because we have been rightly aware of the abstractness and life-estrangement of intellectualistic thinking, we have wrongly assumed that no kind of thinking can be concrete or directly lay hold on life—no thinking is itself alive, able to produce content of its own, able to prove itself as a matter of self-evidence. Yet that intuitive self-evidence in thinking still plays a certain role can be seen, for example, in the reaction of common sense to the biologists' concept of human individuality.

Normal students who hear themselves described as organisms, and try to think of themselves as such, along with all the other organisms being instructed by the teacher organism that is venting its "tissue purposes," will somehow feel overtaken by unreality. They may be nagged by weird questions: "On what 'experimental' evidence do I now base my previously unexamined conviction that I exist? What will suffice to prove that *I am?* Do I fool myself when I think of myself, not as organism at all, but as a fundamentally self-directing, self-sustaining, individuality?" But such students will realize that these questions cannot be determined experimentally in the ordinary sense of that word. The essential fact of *being* can be ascertained only from inside itself, by intuitive self-affirmation.

The power of thought enables us in our own case to experience this intuition of being. And if we can form this intuition concerning ourselves—can realize the "I-*am*" in us—we gain the basis for confidence in the possibility of forming further intuitions about the rest of the world. But when confidence in intuitive experience is lost, every kind of real thinking begins to fade. We come to live less and less actively in our thinking, until we can eventually be persuaded that thinking is only a shadow-work, something that stands outside of the world of reality.

We must develop a new concept of the role of thought. For thought is truly what unites human beings within a common world. As Rudolf Steiner observed in his *Intuitive Thinking as a Spiritual Path:* "In the idea lies the true communion of human beings." When we listen to one another speaking in any social group, it makes no difference whether we are women or men, young or old, rich or poor. The fact is that if the speaker makes an error in logic, we say, "That is false!" Similarly, when a point is soundly made, we say, "That is true!" And we must simply admit what this fact proves: In actively willed thinking we suppress our diversely acculturated individual organisms, in order to allow the clarity of universal reason to hold sway in us; and in and through such active thinking we experience human community.

There is one power of thought amongst all human beings— one mind working in all individual minds. We are separated by our organisms, but we are united to the extent that the universal power of thought thinks itself in us regardless of organic differences. Our unity is achieved not through the common instincts of our animal bodies but through the common light of immaterial thought. Thought is what enables us to go out and enter into things, to penetrate things, and to identify ourselves wholly with them. If we have no confidence in intuitive thinking, the world falls away from us, and we from it. For if we cannot truly know the world, we cannot deeply feel it. When we can no longer care, any motivation to participate creatively must also die.

Western dependence on methods of external proof can be historically justified as having proved fruitful. But historical judgment should also recognize that this forward step has *over-stepped*. Its advantage has long since been pushed to the point of diminishing returns. The doctrinaire experimentalism that once gave science such a boost in exploration of the physical world has now become a roadblock, when the need is to revive the languishing human soul. As we have said, with distrust of clear thinking's ability to go beyond the physical, began the withering away, the atrophy, of thinking itself, and the enfeeblement of other soul forces as well. The first necessity of our time is to achieve a truer concept of the real nature of human thought, for this alone gives the basis for overcoming the unhappy oscillation between blind subjectivism and dead objectivism that has brought so great disorder into education—and through education into every aspect of modern society.

When we come to appreciate that thinking, in its essential nature, transcends both subject and object, we will have found the epistemological basis for a new education. When we realize this fact for certain, we shall be able to make an education that will again place *knowing* at the center of complete human development. In a sense, knowing *can* be the center of education, as traditionalists who call for "basic" education desire. But it can be central only if it can exercise and nourish the whole child, as all forms of progressivism demand. It is not going to involve and satisfy the whole child, however, unless it becomes something more full-fledged than the scientific positivist—the dogmatic experimentalist—presently judges it to be.

We have to realize that in thought there are many levels of cognition. If our thought is superficial, it will give us a superficial picture of the world; if our thought be deeper, it will give us a deeper picture of the world. As much as we put into the act of knowing, that much we shall get out of the reality known. If we fully understand this axiom, we will understand why it is absolutely necessary, even from the viewpoint of a complete and correct science, for the knower's artistic senses, and moral sense as well—for all the soul's powers of feeling and willing—to be used in this *experience* of real knowledge. Our deepest human reactions can no longer be considered irrelevant to the problems of objective knowledge. We must overcome the misunderstanding of the relation between objective fact and what goes on in the human soul as intuitive response, if we are going to present subject matter to children and ask them to "know" it; and yet have them in their knowing be also artistically awakened and morally deepened. Today we have knowing, *and* we have activity. While a clamor of superficial activity draws attention to itself at center stage, real knowing waits like Cinderella in a corner, unrecognized; like Sleeping Beauty in her trance, awaiting deliverance. The renewal of education waits for teachers today who can hew a path through the hedge of thorns that comes between the soul of a student and the spiritual life that should be received from knowledge of the world. So long as the true nature of knowing continues to be dismissed or ignored by teachers, any amount of extra-curricular activities, field trips, problem-solving projects, psychologizing, or social reform around the periphery is not going to make up for the absence of light and warmth right in the middle of the whole educational enterprise. If and when we bring knowledge into its own, we shall not need so much of this peripheral effort; and what we do engage in will be to better effect.

To know a thing intuitively is to *be* the thing. The more we know of the world in this sense, the more fully we shall bring ourselves into existence. Conversely, it is only by coming more fully into existence, with all our capacities of soul, that we can increase this real kind of knowledge. Thus, if we produce a little inward activity with the superficial part of our nature called intellect, we may come to the conception of a mechanical kind of world; but if we further energize, enliven, and ensoul the act of knowing, so as to release our *full* capacity for cognition, the life, soul, and spirit of all that surrounds us will bring us their revelations of reality.

When we realize that humble, loving thought has power actually to participate in all the beings, events, and processes of the world around us, and when we build the goals and methods of teaching upon this realization, we are then glad to bring children to every kind of objective knowledge, for we know that by this very act we shall challenge and awaken their own humanity within them. The art created, and the activities set in motion on the basis of such a knowing, will be human through and through. From them our social life can take new hope.

PART TWO

5

Intellect and the Search for Truth

The soul's advances are not made by gradation, such as can be represented by motion in a straight line, but rather by ascension of state, such as can be represented by metamorphosis—from the egg to the worm from the worm to the fly.

—*Emerson*

THE RELATIONSHIP between human beings as thinkers and the reality about which they think was originally established in a time and mode antedating the appearance of thoughts as we nowadays generally know them. The *feeling* for truth must exist before the *knowledge* of truth. If educators are to develop in children the kind of intuitive intelligence that can penetrate with precision and confidence to the deeper aspects of reality, they will need to realize that properly educated intelligence is born of feeling, and it remains guided by feeling. Without reference to the testimony of feeling, knowledge would not know how to organize itself truthfully. In the search for truth, it would not know, as it were, when it was getting warm and when cold.

Something else, however, antedates even feeling. The feelings about world phenomena that appear in boys and girls during the elementary school years are preceded by what might be called a still more absolute, an even more intimate, experience of reality. Very young children simply yield themselves to what they see. It becomes in them; they become by means of it. This identification takes place more as a matter of inner activity than of feeling, for feeling will come into existence only when a certain gap has begun to open between self and the object encountered—a gap bridged by feeling. But for the youngest child's sense of identification there is no gap. As Whitman wrote—of himself no doubt:

> There was a child went forth every day,
> And the first object he look'd upon, that object he became,
> And that object became part of him . . .

The *gestures* that objects are, become the children's gestures; the will of the one, so to speak, becomes the will of the other. This relationship can be expressed by saying that preschool children are in the highest degree "imitative." Imitation, however, is an inadequate word, easily misunderstood; for it permits one to imagine separation between children and what they imitate. Far from being separate from what they behold, they feel themselves immediately at one with it.

The *truth-sense,* then, actually originates in infancy (or before, according to Plato). That is the time when the child nature "knows" the *being* of what is encountered, and lives immediately within it, in the very act of perception. A physical object as it appears to the adult who looks upon it from the outside may be likened to a frozen wave; but for young children the wave is still in motion, and they are in and of it. Children, in the unconsciousness of their own wills, in the subtle processes of their very lives, know that wave and share its movement.

Before the age of two and a half or so children refer to themselves in the third person, by name. Why do they do this? Because they are, in fact, outside themselves. What are they doing out there? They are living immediately in the objective world. Their consciousness is unfocused because it belongs more to the world as periphery than to themselves as center. Their consciousness is vague because it is comprehensive. It is dim because its light unites with the things it sees, sinking into them instead of playing brightly upon them from outside.

During elementary school years, children *begin* to separate themselves from the world. They nevertheless still feel its tides. They are still moved by objects and events as they were in the preschool years, if less so. What is a less in immediate identity, however, becomes a more somewhere else; namely, in the development of that mediate relationship we call feeling.

Elementary grade children have withdrawn a step from a sense of identity with the outer world, but they have therefore begun to open a capacity inside themselves for their partly separate experience. They show an inward power of *feeling* that preschool children do not yet have. They vividly react toward people and things, but are less absolutely captured by such encounters. The inclusive-pervasive atmosphere of feeling now arises between these children and the world. On the one hand, they live close enough to reality for the life of each being they encounter to stir them. On the other hand, they are distant enough to respond in imagination rather than action. Because at this age children are not yet *fully* internalized as *subject*, the world for them has not fully externalized itself into *objects*. They and their environment are mingled, as we have said, in the half-internal, half-external drama of feeling.

With adolescence, the self grows still more inward and more "spiritual," while the not-self further externalizes or materializes itself. The gap between the two widens, and the bridge of feeling is threatened with collapse. These days the collapse generally takes place, because during the elementary years, most methods of education, since they do not give importance to feeling, have not permitted it to establish and strengthen itself. At this point, therefore, young people tend to perceive hard facts in the world outside themselves, and within themselves think abstract thoughts. Within these thoughts their sense of self fully wakes up for the first time, but the outer world has withdrawn its reality from them. World-*being*, we may say, has died into world-*fact*. The world-*presence*, with which children normally feel themselves intimately related during the years when their consciousness was larger but less centered, is now laid out before their diminished self as the enigmatic mask of world-*appearance*.

In this third stage of development during the adolescent years, when young adults begin to live in thoughts, everything depends on the nature of these thoughts. Their quality will depend upon how they have been built up from earliest childhood. If children's teachers have ignored will and feeling, and from kindergarten forward have directed their attention primarily to intellect, both their ability to think and their enjoyment of thought will have been reduced. They will regard thoughts themselves as mere negatives of reality. Not only will such thoughts be unable to direct the course of events, giving purpose to life and holding life to that purpose; not only will they fail to please the soul, leaving it empty and querulous; but they will scarcely maintain themselves even as thought-forms. There will be weakness in the will to search out the truth, weakness in the feeling for such truth as they find, and eventually weakness in maintaining even the barest outlines of the concepts through which truth speaks.

If, on the other hand, parents and teachers in the earliest years have educated primarily through the will, and thereafter during the elementary years primarily through feeling, before making demands directly upon the intellect—so that will and feeling have been successively strengthened as such—then truth-seeking will come at last into its own. It will prove to be the fulfillment of will and the fulfillment of feeling. A dynamic and heart-felt power for clear thinking will serve to arrive at well-founded truth. The thinker will then realize inward satisfaction as well as outward objectivity.

To distinguish between thought as fading subjective construct and thought as dawning expression of objective, full-fledged reality, is to lay bare the essential difference between what we have called intellect and intuitive intelligence, or between intellect with an anemic, and intellect with a robust, sense of truth. The thoughts that have started in early childhood as active absorption into the environment, and gone on during the elementary years to become articulated feelings with and about things, flower at last as living ideas. These are the content of real intelligence. In them, the original power of identification, which is greatest in infancy, through right feeling, still directs the search for truth. It is just this continuing capacity for innermost identification and realization that makes of mature thought a homing pigeon.

6

The Experience of Knowledge

... a mysterious force of gravity which determines that a jour-
ney into the unknown in the world without produces a movement towards new and unknown areas in our world within.
There is a profound interdependence of world without and
world within, and experience in either one of them is valid
also in the other. Whenever one succeeds in breaking the code
wherein their meaning is transmitted from one dimension to
the other, this validity is so marked that one wonders whether
they are really two different dimensions and not just two aspects of one and the same whole. The visible world being
merely the spirit seen from without; the spirit, just the world
without seen from within. —*Sir Laurens van der Post*

TO BRING ABOUT THE FULL USE of intelligence, so that the
educated person will also be capable and truly human, Waldorf
schools throughout the world have developed a unique method. This method, running through a twelve-year curriculum, is
based on Rudolf Steiner's theory of knowledge and on his psychology of child development. It makes the gaining of knowledge a completely human experience. I shall try to describe the
method and consequences of Waldorf education from this
viewpoint.

The decline in the prestige, power, and practicality of human
intelligence was already well along, and its consequences could
be clearly foreseen, when in 1919 Rudolf Steiner established
the curriculum and methods of the first Waldorf school in
Stuttgart, Germany. Steiner hoped through a new form of education to develop the kind of intelligence that would again inspire confidence. In this way he could contribute to rebuilding

the health of contemporary society. Since 1919, over six hundred Waldorf schools have sprung up in Europe, the United Kingdom, Africa, and South America.[1]

Sound intelligence cannot be developed apart from a balanced care for all faculties of the human soul; and conversely, these other capacities for experience and achievement will not bear fruit properly unless intelligence has come into its own. Since the knowledge with which education confronts children and young people consists primarily of facts to be observed and ideas to be thought, such observations and thoughts must be handled in ways that will touch and move young people where they truly live. These ways of teaching must discipline as they deepen subjective response. In seeking to develop the cognitive power that lies hidden in feeling and will, Waldorf teachers use the very methods that encourage psychological and moral response, enabling them to advance rather than obstruct the search for real knowledge.

How can teaching cause the objective content of mathematics, science, social studies, and the language arts to humanly touch and move students? Let us take a few examples, starting at the first grade, to show what a difference it makes when teachers use the materials of their subjects to evoke inner activity in their pupils.

READING: Generally, the great goal of first grade is that children learn to read. But *early* reading is less important than *really* reading. True reading begins with a vivid experience of the creative, formative powers that lie within language. This means that the immediate sounds and shapes of language must be

---

1. As of 1994 there were over six hundred schools in almost forty countries. Hans-Joachim Mattke, ed. *Waldorf Education World-Wide: Celebrating the 75th Anniversary of the Uhlandschöhe Waldorf School in Stuttgart*, Offizin Chr. Scheufele, Stuttgart, 1994.

made interesting; they must come to have overtones and under-tones, as well as meaningful associations. Teachers call upon their imaginations to present the letters of the alphabet as active personalities. Already in this first moment, they use a method that helps children learn to read not only primers, but eventually also the language of nature and of human life itself.

Teachers who would read the book of life, and teach their pupils to read it, must appreciate that the world as it appears before our physical eyes is only half real. The most important part is physically imperceptible, even as the meaning of words is imperceptible. The letters as spelled do not supply the meaning as read. The leap from letters to meaning—meaning that has value for the human heart and mind—requires that in observing facts we look away from substance to form. By analogy, it is as though in listening to our friends, we subordinate our mental grasp of the content and logic of what they are saying to something more intimate and deeper. We listen with open heart—specifically, to *how* they speak: to the intonation, timbre, pace, and emphasis, to the sculpture, music, and color, of their speaking. We listen with inner ears to the *form* of speech, and in so listening we receive far more than information or argument. We come into touch with all that moves and lives within the souls of our friends.

The leap from mere spelling in our observations about life to intuitive comprehension demands that we learn to see the form of each fact or event as a meaningful gesture; that we sense that it is expressing something in dramatic fashion; and that we begin, however obscurely, to feel what this something is. Proceeding in this way, we move from a quickened interest in forms to the intuition that each of these forms has character and reveals character. But when we have come so far, we are mightily stirred and awakened, for we feel ourselves no longer as outsiders looking on at a world of material facts and processes, but as souls who know they have the possibility of being insiders. We are on the threshold of experiencing the world as a great animate Presence. Through the gate of form we find our way into Being.

Goethe said, "All that is passing is but a parable." This is to say that the produced forms of the material world are but the masks of underlying, productive spiritual realities. Steiner held it essential for all education, though especially for education during the elementary school years, that

> all perception must be spiritualized. We ought not to be satisfied, for instance, with presenting a plant, a seed, a flower to the child merely as it can be perceived with the senses. Everything should become a parable of the spiritual. In a grain of corn there is far more than meets the eye. There is a whole new plant invisible within it. That such a thing as a seed has more within it than can be perceived with the senses, this the child must grasp in a living way with feeling and imagination. A child must, in feeling, divine the secrets of existence. The objection cannot be made that the pure perception of the senses is obscured by this means; on the contrary, by going no further than what the senses see, we are stopping short of the whole truth. For the full reality consists of the spirit as well as the substance; and there is no less need for faithful and careful observation when one is bringing all the faculties of the soul into play, than when only the physical senses are employed. . . . Of what good is it in the highest sense, that children should have shown to them all possible varieties of minerals, plants and animals, and all kinds of physical experiments, if something further is not bound up with the teaching of these things; namely, to make use of the parables that the sense-world gives, to awaken a feeling for the secrets of the spirit? (*The Education of the Child*, pp. 41-2)

To make the abstract conventionalized letters of the alphabet come alive for first graders is a first step on the way to bringing all else to life. We shall try to show that this art has its own laws and necessities. It is not to be confused with cheap tricks and shallow excitements. The deeper meanings that are to be read in nature, in history, and even in the alphabet, can be suggested through the free use of imagination, yet they must not be in any way mere fantasies. They must be really there. From this requirement comes everything that is needed to discipline both teacher and child.

Waldorf schools do not waste much time debating the respective values of the sight and sound methods of reading. They use both, and more besides. But their uniqueness lies in the way they release the inherent power of the miraculous word from the humdrum of conventional speaking, writing, and reading. First of all, the stories they tell in the earliest grades are not trivialities drawn from middle-class existence but enduring tales of imagination: fairy tales, fables, myths, legends. And these stories are not at first read by the teacher from books, but are freshly reconstructed in the telling. This immediately creative act of shaping the spoken word makes a much deeper impression than reading aloud. It commands the students' full attention, because the teacher's whole human force is in it. The stories, furthermore, serve as more than a temporary excuse for practicing an academic skill. They are an end in themselves, in their beauty and lasting wonder, in their moral force, and in the fact that they contain the ripened wisdom of the human race. Children are enlivened and nourished by such stories, whether or not they immediately learn from them how to read. Artistic sense, moral sense, the capacity to experience life's deeper realities, are given content to work upon.

While listening to the great stories that have guided humanity through the centuries, children know at once why they have come to school. What they meet there imparts fresh life to their blood and breathing. They are eager to spend this life in creative endeavor. The next step is to express what they have felt, to continue it into flowing color, into speech or song or bodily movement. Intellectual understanding comes last of all, and gradually at that; for the full understanding of what lies in fairy tale, myth, fable, and legend will hardly be compassed in a lifetime.

By comparison, the repetitive working over of stories whose content is exhausted in the first encounter (and whose only excuse for being lies in the fact that they afford exercise in the few hundred "most used" but not necessarily most amusing or colorful words of the language) must be accounted unrewarding.

If the aim is to be the fullest *experience* of knowledge, one realizes that reading should not precede but should follow the practice of writing. First comes the action, always; then the recognition. First through movement and speech, then through writing of the spoken word, language is created. Through hearing and through reading, it is perceived. In life generally, creation comes first and then the beholding, the onlooking, the appreciation. So, according to Genesis, the world itself once evolved, having been first divine creative presence and activity, and only at the end of each "day" a thing apart, that divine consciousness could look upon and find "good."

THE ALPHABET: The way a Waldorf school teacher approaches teaching the letters of the alphabet to first graders is characteristic of the art of education These shapes and sounds are placed before the children as things interesting, in and of themselves. First of all, the letters are there to be delighted in for the quality of their sounding. Each sound brings forth its telling form. Once appreciated in this way, the friendly alphabet becomes the foundation of good handwriting and of the whole art of language.

Thus, letters like *B, M, P,* or *S,*[2] will fill the room with sound, and will be put on paper with loving care, in color, using great strokes. They will be painted large with fantasy before being drawn small in the conventional style. The shape of the letter B for instance, may be extracted from a memorable story about a bumblebee, or a butterfly, or a bear. This B retains in its form something of the burgeoning, blooming, bountiful things of which it speaks. The children quickly sense the relationship. They will do the walking, dancing, or modeling of B, and the painting, drawing, and writing of it, out of a sense for the formative quality that lives both in its given shape and in its shaping sound. The sounding of B will be dramatic. No prosaic repetitions of "bee is for B" in a business-as-usual tone of the voice. No sitting and saying, repeating and memorizing, of colorless phonics. Rather, the welling up in children as they speak of a vivid force that makes them burly, brawny, big—or blessed, beaming, and beautiful—as the sound accumulates in their limbs, in their chests, and in the breath behind their lips. The B will be found again and again, of course, in bells and balls and bows and baskets, for the force it pictures is one of the burgeoning shapers of creation. Of quite incidental importance at first will be the fact that B is a standardized sign that must be learned if one is to read.

In the letter P first graders can see, once their attention is called to it, how the form shows a pressure that rises to ever new heights. The embrace of B becomes the presumption, pride, or mounting power of P. As the water rises ever upward in a "pump," so the flow of pride and power arises in "pomp" or, more mildly, in "papa." Peacocks and pouter pigeons, and the plume in a cavalier's hat, seem written in the world as P's. A lesser

---

2. The consonants should be pronounced as far as possible without vowel sounds being added. The final *ee* sound that is conventional usage does not really belong to the B itself, any more than to a P or T or Z.

potency, but of the same quality, we find in "pout" (hear and see the perpetual pouting of "s-pouts") or "pamper." Imagine the rising curiosity, the standing on tiptoes, of those who "pry" and "poke" and "peek" into things, in pursuit of possible knowledge.

The world contains in its shapes all the other consonants, too. We see in M mountains, in V, a valley between the peaks. Observe a person's upper lip. The mouth is an original M; and as the lips press mildly, warmly together, humming is felt as a vibration of M in "mama," "milk," "mix," and "mingle."

R tumbles from P's eminence. R runs, is rapid, races in rings. See its mobile shape! Hear it running in "cur-rr-ent," and "tr-r-avel," and the "pur-r-ring" of the "motor-r-r car-rr."

F is a fleet one of another kind. Fish flash through the water, as birds flit and flicker through the air. If teachers are free souls in following their fancies, they can conjure a mood in the classroom that will make pupils see the conventional F as derived from a flowing, and this in turn as concealed in the body of the fish, of the flying bird, and the flickering flames of every fire.

Experience of the shaping power of the miraculous letters of the alphabet—which in their combinations are capable of expressing all the facts and moods of the world—is pursued in Waldorf schools much further in the ways indicated here. Rudolf Steiner's new art of movement, called eurythmy, is a kind of "visible speech" used to develop objective feeling for the movements inherent in language. Eurythmy is supported in turn by the effort to speak so clearly and positively that "phonetic values" rise from the grave of conventional speech as living forces.

As we have said, children educated in this way gain more than the use of reading as a tool. They gain access to the inspiration that makes poets. They are close to the marvel of how the human soul could ever in the first place have coined world events into language, and then into thought. They will be able one day to sense the truth which lies behind the otherwise inexplicable statement that "In the beginning of all things was the creative Word," for the world of created beings is a divine utterance, and human speech only imitates its language of forms.[3] The teaching of reading in a Waldorf school rests, then, upon the unspoken premise that *all* the world's forms are expressive gestures that may be read, if we but learn how. First grade is the time to begin this learning, by experiencing the alphabet.

The simplest detail at this earliest stage suffices for drama. Let us suppose the teacher wishes to convey the introductory thought that all printing is but combinations of curved and straight lines. Everything will depend upon what the teacher is able to make of the concepts "straight" and "curved." We can present these ideas by the very way we stand and move as we speak of these two forms, or by drawing them on the blackboard; and the children can realize they are dealing with two radically different kinds of activity: one that makes things strictly, absolutely straight, and another that turns forever, without so much as a hint of straightness to mar its vital arcs. The practice of alternately drawing straight and curved lines, or running them on the floor of the gymnasium, will become an exercise of the child's whole being. How educational this exercise is will be obvious from the intellectual child's struggle to produce true curves and the emotional child's difficulty in drawing a straight line.

ARITHMETIC: The concept of numbers given to first graders must be simple, but not trivial. Even something as abstract

---

3. I am here discussing the consonants only. Vowels, in Steiner's opinion, are not imitations of the outer forms or gestures of things so much as expressions of human feelings in response to forms. This difference being understood, vowels can be taught in an equally real way.

as pure number can be artistically, morally, and humanly experienced.[4] The number 1, for example, is not primarily a unit made for acquisitive stockpiling. *It is itself the sum*—any sum, every sum. It contains within itself treasure to be bestowed, shared, divided. The original and originating completeness of any whole is 1—unity before it has evolved opposition from within itself. "We live in one world, this is one class, you belong to one family. Despite your many teeth and fingers and toes, you are one child. . . ." Integrity and perfection are to be found in 1.

The teacher breaks 1 stick, or cuts 1 piece of paper, to show the origin of 2. This gesture is dramatic; it can even be distressing. More is revealed about the essential nature of 2 when it is introduced thus as a division of 1 than when it is built up out of two 1's. 2 stands for all the polarities, oppositions, and contrasts of which the manifest world is composed: for light and darkness, the heights and depths, summer and winter, wet and dry, inside and out, past and future, positive and negative, man and woman. Were it not for the saving 3, evolution from oneness to duality would be a disaster!

How greatly we can admire, then, the nature of 3, which contains the mystery of how antagonistic forces can be harnessed for progress, and how we hold our path of moral choice

---

4. "Plato writes in the *Epinomis* that among all the liberal arts and contemplative sciences, the science of numbering is supreme and most divine. And in another place, asking why man is the wisest of animals, he replies, because he knows how to count. Similarly, Aristotle, in his *Problems* repeats this opinion. Abumasar writes that it was a favorite saying of Avenzoar of Babylon that the man who knows how to count, knows everything else as well. These opinions are certainly devoid of any truth if by the art of number they intend that art in which today merchants excel all other men. . . ."—Giovanni Pico Della Mirandola, *Oration on the Dignity of Man.*

between the contrasting temptations that beset us from one side and from the other. 3 is father-mother-child. In standing *here* we represent 3, because we do not stand above or below, to the right or left, to the front or back, of here. And equally we celebrate the 3 by living *now*: not in the past, not in the future. Though teachers will scarcely tell their young charges all the reasons why, they will accord deepest respect to the triad, for through it teachers will have looked into many a wonder of how the world is organized.

Quality can be found in numbers 1, 2, and 3 as well as quantity. So with every number. It is important that teachers find the way to bring pupils to a qualitative experience of at least some numbers. Further progress in this direction may be made when, somewhat later, they point out that though 5 times 2 is 10, and 2 times 5 is 10, these two 10's are in one sense unlike, since five 2's are qualitatively not the same thing at all as two 5's. Geometrical figures also prove helpful in reinforcing the experience of numbers. 1 may be a circle. 2 may be parallel lines that will never meet. 3 will be a triangle, 4 a square, 5 a pentagram or star, 6 the cells in a honeycomb.

Thus, one way of describing the fundamental method of Waldorf education is to say that it rests upon the premise that the character of the world-process as a whole is in some sense to be found again in each fact and event of that process. Each particular fact therefore has been struck rightly by the teacher when the student can hear it resounding as a tone with overtones and world-echoes. This method does not ask teachers to philosophize or point morals, for that would be ill-suited to children. Neither does it demand that they themselves be conscious of the *ultimate* implications of the facts presented, for that would be impossible. It does, however, require the teacher to develop an unusual aptitude for seeing much in little.

It is not necessary to review an entire curriculum through twelve grades in order to show how the learning of each fact, idea, and skill may become a full human experience. Yet a few more examples chosen from the curriculum of older children will perhaps suggest that an appropriate point of view gradually enables any teacher to discover methods to this end. Let us consider the teaching of the social and natural sciences.

HISTORY: In Waldorf schools, history is studied beginning at the fifth grade. Before that, history has been prepared for in third, fourth, and early fifth grades by mythology. Myths relating how the gods first brought cosmic nature into being, and how the arts of civilization were established by legendary culture heroes—these myths are to be found, for example, in Genesis, the Eddas, the *Rigveda* and *Ramayana, the Zendavesta,* Plutarch's story of Isis and Osiris, Hesiod's *Theogony* and the Homeric *Hymns.* These are not only great literature welcomed by children at this age, they also lay the basis for an understanding of the religious traditions and folk psychology that help to explain much of later history. These myths are told, read, written, illustrated, and dramatized; but they are not explained, much less explained away. The purpose is to have children live again briefly through what humankind once experienced in the various stages of its youth. Young people have an instinctive understanding for the reality of true myth; and they come into the fully modern realities a little later with more self-possession and greater impetus, if they have had the chance to share in what has gone before. Also, when given some grounding in the intuitive conceptions of the past, they will be less imprisoned by the limitations of our present mode of thinking, as they enter it: rather, they will be ready for the new ways of looking at things that the future, if it is to transcend the present, must bring.

To make history live for students, nothing can be more helpful than the realization that human history expresses an evolution of consciousness. Each period of culture becomes understandable, therefore, only to the extent that we can imagine vividly the state of mind from which it issued. Every newly emerging change of consciousness has brought corresponding developments in religion, the arts, social relationships, government, and economic activity. To have students *experience* the knowledge of history, therefore, is to awaken in them the kind of inner attitude, the psychological capacities, that originally made each culture and civilization what it was.

One must recognize that in the course of its evolution through succeeding epochs human consciousness has developed certain aptitudes by losing others. Therefore the modern tendency to look with contempt upon the past is understandable. Yet it cannot be condoned. Should the infant who bears manifold inner potentialities be judged inferior to the adult that the infant later becomes—and who will have realized but some fragment of the infant's early possibilities at the expense of all the rest? Human scientific knowledge and prowess today are truly extraordinary, yet in studying ancient cultures without prejudice one learns that at their best they made up in a comprehensive wisdom for what they lacked of our complicated knowledge of detail; they made up with spiritual power for what they lacked of our material powers.

In trying to make history a real experience for pupils, teachers must strive continually, as we have said, to improve the ability to read the language of form. It was so in the first grade with the numbers and the letters of the alphabet. It should be so in the teaching of history from fifth grade on. Teachers will treat historical cultures symptomatically, as it were, and with an artist's eye for style. In reviewing the literature, architecture, tools, religious institutions, or social customs of an epoch, students will feel themselves being stirred and shaped when they attempt to live into the kind of consciousness these forms reveal. Thus they are given the key to history.

In the lower grades of a Waldorf school the teaching of history tries, through building up the drama of critical events and key personalities, to induce an imaginative identification with other epochs, moving from ancient times toward the modern age. The teaching of history in high school covers the same ground more systematically, now aiming to distill laws and reasons out of the feelings established the first time through. This is always the sequence in Waldorf education: first the immediately moving experience, then the quiet ripening of this experience—usually helped by working it through in one art form or another—and finally the crystallization of concepts. The more fundamentally the original experience is anchored in the student, the more productive of ideas one expects it to be as time goes on.

As Waldorf teachers see it, the study of history should be an experience of the evolving nature of time; for time appears to have content in and of itself, to be qualitatively differentiated.[5] The problem, therefore, is to help children loosen themselves from contemporary attitudes, so that they may discover the unique qualities of earlier times. This is not difficult if the epochs of history are taught in a certain correspondence with the children's own psychological development. The study of Greece, for example, is perfect for fifth grade, when childhood

---

5. "For most of us time is only a 'when,' a linear current measured by the ticking of clocks over which it flows like water over a wheel, a measure completely at our disposal and according to which we make dates and keep our business appointments. We are so caught up in this linear movement that we never stop to consider that time may also have content and nature, a specific meaning of its own which makes it not merely a 'when' but also a 'what' and perhaps, more important still, also a 'how' and a 'way to eternity.'" —Sir Laurens van der Post, *The Dark Eye in Africa.*

is most in balance.[6] By early sixth grade, when reason begins to take hold and individuality to consolidate, children are ready for Rome. Usually in Waldorf schools, sixth grade carries the story on into the Middle Ages; for the children's thinking is now ready to test its own subtlety, and the pre-adolescent soul to begin its quest for the ideal. By seventh grade, when boys and girls feel new power within themselves, when they are ready to set aside traditional authority, in order to freely explore wider horizons of every kind—in science, in human relationships, in practical undertakings—they bring intuitive understanding to the Renaissance, the Reformation, and the beginnings of modern times. And then in eighth and ninth grades, when physical maturity supports a certain here-and-now outlook, the time comes to bring history fully up to date. The high school years repeat the earlier sequence, but in a new way, starting once again with ancient history and ending with modern.

GEOGRAPHY: If history explores time, geography explores space. Geography is well taught when it awakens the human experiences that are appropriate to the differentiations of earthly space. One cannot speak of seas and mountains and plains as though they were exclusively physical and economic facts. There is also the distinctive spirit of place. People who live on or by the sea do not have the same experience as those who live among mountains. Thus, to say merely that the

---

6. "What is the foundation of that interest all men feel in Greek history, letters, art and poetry.... What but this, that every man passes personally through a Grecian period.... The student interprets the age of chivalry by his own age of chivalry, and the days of maritime adventure and circumnavigation by quite parallel miniature experiences of his own. To the sacred history of the world he has the same key."—Ralph Waldo Emerson, *History.*

mountaineer's life differs from the sailor's because the economy of the former is built on forestry and mining while that of the latter rests upon fishing and commerce, is true; but it describes only external factors. Yet to try for more psychological depth by saying that mountaineers and sailors both have strong characters because both are exposed to weather, to solitude, and to danger, still does not bring us to the nub of the matter. If the experience of knowledge is to have exactitude, the psychological facts of geography should be as specifically *felt* as the physical facts are *known*.

Is not the contrast between mountain and sea a cause as well as an image of deep contrasts in the moral experience of humankind? Mountains define, but by the same act they also divide. They teach integrity but may go further, to instill antipathy. By the climbing of mountains we are elevated above ordinary life, but we may also be alienated from it. Certainty of thought and intensity of purpose we do acquire from mountains; when these go too far, however, they become dogmatism or quarrelsomeness.

The sea, by contrast, moderates irritability, levels differences, teaches us sympathy—if it does not go further to lose us in vast uncertainty, confounding us in the equivocal, or stupefying us with dreams. Sailing Earth's seas, we can learn largeness of heart; from its swells we can absorb the power of rhythm; looking to the perfect horizon we can find composure. Transposed to literary terms, is not the difference between sea and mountain the same as that between the writing of Melville or Whitman and that of Emerson or Thoreau?

The result of limited imagination in the teaching of geography can be seen in the attitude many people nowadays adopt toward ocean travel, toward flying, and toward mountain climbing. The typical person usually anticipates little, experiences little, enjoys the movement and change, and is stimulated by the physical challenges. But people are scarcely open to the specific wonder of each of the elements to which we consign ourselves. Mechanization of transport—and of mental attitudes—has made traveling up mountains by motorized chairlift, across the ocean by ship engines, and through the air by airplane engines, all more and more like one another. Modernly educated human beings are hardly prepared or able to make the most of what confronts them. They do not adapt themselves readily to the special occasion, as it were, but reduce all occasions to uniformity, thereby insulating themselves more and more successfully from the inspiration particular environments offer those who are awake and in touch.

Ancient peoples felt how the ascent of a mountain brings one who is prepared into progressively rarefied regions. Because they climbed mountains with inner as well as outer activity, they achieved an enhancement of experience that is generally missed by modern climbers who remain preoccupied with the physical trials and the challenge to the ego. The inspiration of the airy heights, where ancient peoples sensed the dwelling of their gods, is all but closed off today by banality of mind that begins in school. Openness to this experience can be renewed by right teaching. And what is true for mountains is equally true for the experience of springs and rivers, of tundra and jungle, of volcanic eruption, typhoon, and earthquake. Each has its own mystery.

Earth, water, air, and fire form our environment. Each should bring us unique experiences. If the air cannot release and uplift us, will drugs do it? If the water cannot heal and quiet us, will tranquilizers do it? If direct contact with Earth's granite cannot consolidate our strength, will psychoanalysis or vitamin pills succeed?

CULTURAL GEOGRAPHY: The study of *economic* geography is first taken up by Waldorf schools in grades four through six. Cultural geography is added to economic in grades seven through ten. The study of cultural traits from a geographic point of view leads to the experience that north, south, east, and west are not merely compass readings, but psychological functions of the Earth organism.

Remarkably enough, there is a north-south polarity to be experienced not only on Earth as a whole, but in each country. North and south tend to divide any given land between themselves, imprinting their natures respectively upon customs, speech, dress, disposition. In the northern hemisphere, north is, of course, relatively the land of winter. Its gesture is one of taciturnity and terseness; of frugality, patience, and inner strengthening. In the south, where summer reigns, people live more at the surface of themselves, as may be observed in the limber gait of southern peoples, their graceful manners, ready flow of speech, and easy hospitality, not to mention other qualities enumerated long ago by Vitruvius, in his instruction to architects who wish to build in ways really appropriate to climate and climatic temperament.

Earth's spring, summer, fall, and winter, and the geographical regions that typify them, are further experienced when the contrasting effects of each upon growth and consciousness have been appreciated: in spring and in the south, the rising growth-forces and submergence of wakefulness; in fall and in northerly regions, the inhibition of growth, with resurgence of mental activity. Children in the upper elementary grades are able to make much of such contrasts, using them as clues to a deeper understanding of cultural facts.

Earth's east and west and middle are not only places, but powers. They mold consciousness as well as style of life. Such style may be found in the characteristics of flora and fauna as well as in people's habits. For example, how the Far East, Middle Europe, and the West are related to one another culturally can be suggested by the teacher who knows how to describe the growing conditions and the physical appearance of the three cereal plants that have been for so long their characteristic staffs of life: rice, wheat, and corn. It is of extraordinary interest that the staple grain of the East is planted in water, and that the kernels of its head spread out delicately into the air from the uppermost part of the graceful stalk. American maize, at the other extreme, is close to the solid earth. Its kernels are tough and crude. They are tightly packed on a bulky cob. The cobs issue from the sides of a heavy stalk. The waterborne, somewhat ethereal rice seems fit for a more contemplative people. The rugged, earthbound maize belongs to quite another system of forces. And European wheat, oats, and rye, whose heads are not so extended as those of rice yet much less compacted than the corncob, may be felt to hold the balance between East and West.[7]

Today we speak much of how to increase understanding between the peoples of the Earth. This understanding will remain purely mental, however—that is, helpless to control international relationships—unless it penetrates to the will. Only when various peoples and places, even directions of the compass, are intuitively, forcefully, *realized* in personal experience, may we hope that social studies will contribute to the actual achievement of world peace.

FOREIGN LANGUAGES: The difference between theoretical good will and real attunement as the basis for international understanding may be seen in the attitudes schools adopt toward language teaching. At the present time many parents would like their schools to begin the study of one or more

---

7. For a study of cultural differences between the East, the West, and Middle Europe, see *National Psychology in International Relations, by* Franz E. Winkler, M.D., published by the Myrin Institute, Inc., 521 Park Avenue, New York, N.Y. 10021.

foreign languages in the elementary grades; but the reasons for this wish sometimes differ from those which for over seventy years have induced Waldorf schools to teach two modern languages besides the native tongue to all students from kindergarten through the eighth grade.

A popular thought is that children exposed to foreign languages in the elementary school are getting a head start. They are acquiring not only a symbol of prestige, but a useful tool for business or politics later on. Yet, as some realists point out, there are reasons why early language study may neither save time for the language student in high school, nor pay off financially in later life. And as for improving international amity, these skeptics maintain, more would be accomplished by having children spend precious school hours on studies of a particular nation's history, economy, and so on, than by having them memorize its vocabulary, syntax, and grammar.

But all this misses the main point of what the early study of languages can accomplish. When the teacher's direct method of presentation is met by the artistic sensibilities that are natural in very young students, the sounds, idioms, and constructions of a language are deeply experienced. The soul of a nation is said to live in its language, and through the language this soul penetrates the children born to the nation. It conforms them to itself. Something of the same effect takes place if this language is learned by a foreigner during the openhearted years of early childhood. Character is fundamentally altered thereby. Provincialism is attacked at its root. The result for any children lucky enough to have been well exposed to a foreign language is that, even if they forget the particular language later on, or find that they must eventually deal with quite other countries than the one whose language has been experienced, they will retain a gift for sympathetic insight and tact. The fact that they learned to think and feel in more ways than one will help them to a certain magnanimity. The flexibility gained in the very structure of the mind through the modifying experience of foreign languages studied early on will be more successful in preparing a person to cope with the ways of other cultures than theoretical tolerance or abstract knowledge could ever be.

NATURAL SCIENCE: To make knowledge of the natural sciences also a matter of experience requires the same methods that are fruitful in languages, the social studies, mathematics. One asks students to *observe*, but one also lets them wait for the observation to sink in. When their feelings are moved, they are allowed a certain amount of time in which to grow and sort themselves out, before an attempt is made to extract concise ideas from them.

Botany, for example, is generally stressed in Waldorf schools in fifth grade, and it appears again in the high school. Botanical studies and observations, of course, bring students definite conceptions of the structure and development of plants. But this knowledge would remain as lifeless as any other, even though plants represent life itself, were not the growing and changing of the plant to occur also in the student. For this purpose physical observation and intellectual analysis do not suffice. Imagination is essential, and this imagining must partake also of the nature of moral experience.

Imagination makes the observed metamorphosis of plants — from the comparatively crude, more fleshy lower leaf to the delicate, more serrated upper leaf; from opaque green leaves to almost transparent petals of many colors; from the expanded corolla to the concentrated pistil and stamen; from these, by expansion again, to fruit, and then by contraction to seed—into actual experiences of life. Goethe showed that the leaf nature as it rises above the earth into light and warmth undergoes not only physical changes of form, but qualitative enhancement. It enters higher stages of existence. It is able to express ever more of itself under the more refined conditions encountered and achieved as it climbs upwards. Aspects of itself that were concealed within the earlier stages come to view: the beautiful colors, the perfected forms; the clarity, warmth, and perfume of flowers; the savors and sugar of fruits. Such marvels of metamorphosis awaken faculties beyond the intellectual in students who attempt to follow them inwardly.

A knowledge limited to the structures and "mechanisms" of plant-growth is useful if one wishes to transform the kingdom of life conceptually into a machine, in order to gain control of this machine for technical uses. But if we have no wish to pull life down to mechanics, we must overcome the mechanized thinking that exerts such a strong influence on our minds today. Above all, we must enliven the capacity for knowing. Then we can know life as *life:* we shall not only *know* that plants are *alive,* but this knowledge will be an actual sharing in that life. Teachers who have conveyed to students at some time even a single pulsebeat of life itself, as Waldorf teachers certainly try to do, will have set their hand on the door that opens to creative inspiration of every kind.

What has been said of botany is true of zoology, of mineralogy, of meteorology. The outer event is used to waken the corresponding inner event. When Waldorf school children study animals in fourth grade, they are still young enough to feel at once how foxy is the fox, with the large intelligent ears, the exquisitely sharp nose, the dainty feet, the floating tail that seems formed of air and light. They have memorable experiences at the zoo and in the museum of natural history, when they look into the eyes of wolf or owl or alligator. Even earlier, in second grade, Aesop's fables have brought many an animal into the classroom in such a way that the children could slip readily into its skin. As the years go by, there are other opportunities—

especially, of course, in high school zoology—for each species of animal to make its unique impression. In high school, the study has its detailed, analytical, and classificatory aspects; but these need not block experience. Indeed, they should intensify it.

Children who can feel the lion's prowess, the cow's contentment, and the eagle's lofty spirit awakening in themselves will become interesting and capable people. Imitative, imaginative, and intuitive familiarity with animal styles and behavior will make children wise also in the ways of people.

The more children can learn to harmonize their own inward gesture and mood with what they encounter outside themselves, the less chance there is they will grow up to appear educated yet actually remain unawakened. Goethe said, "Every object rightly seen unlocks a new faculty of the soul," yet for many people education has unlocked very little. It has trained them to look at every object not "rightly," which would mean devoting patient attention to the object until it begins to live in them and they in it and each observation makes them a new person; but "objectively," which means with an external attitude, they remaining the same regardless of what is observed. No amount of objective power that may be won over nature by technical means will ever compensate for the subjective boredom, the pernicious anemia of soul, that result for the knower who so limits her or his knowing. The least of natural processes deserves the student's complete presence of mind. The boiling of water, the reflection of light, the burning of metals, can all become aesthetic and moral experiences of great importance for the whole of life.

Since every student in a Waldorf high school is required to take physics and chemistry as well as biology, these sciences must all have something to give to the individual whose preoccupation is more artistic or ethical than scientific. Laboratory experiments can have this universal appeal if the experiment is made as dramatic as possible, and if the teacher allows the drama of the demonstration to sink in before coming to the technical "explanation," which, though necessary, ordinarily remains for the inner human being something comparatively trivial. Whether a gas is being heated, a pendulum swung, a lever or screw put to work, the teacher demonstrates in the same spirit that is expected of the students: namely, one of reverence and anticipation, as of a great wonder. The deed is allowed to speak for itself. The event is embedded in an attentive silence. Somewhat rapt observation is followed by descriptive review and the commentary of human reactions, before technical comment begins—perhaps the next day. Time is allowed for the observed event to inscribe itself upon memory and be carried through sleep. In this way, it can make its full impression upon the student, before his or her mind narrows to the conventional task of scanning it for physical laws.

As the fire warms the water, the physics teacher would also like to have it warm something in the student. When the bubbles begin to form on the bottom of the vessel, the same event ought to be taking place within the student—with amazement and delight, and perhaps even some pain. Every such physical event stands as the perfect expression of some moral experience, even as each moral experience gives the inner reality of an external event to be discovered somewhere in the world. Outer and inner belong to each other. The progress of true knowing consists in realizing the moments of this correspondence.[8]

Understandably, many teachers today do not recognize that the world-content has something to give, through completely

---

8. "O Nature, and O soul of man! how far beyond all utterances are your linked analogies; not the smallest atom stirs or lives on matter, but has its cunning duplicate in mind."—Herman Melville, *Moby Dlck*.

experienced thought, to every part and power of the human soul. Their training has not led them to appreciate that within each fact the apparent world conceals many levels of truth, and that each of these truths requires from us its particular form of active, inward response.[9] This insight, however, was the source of the wisdom Waldorf school teachers prize so much in an earlier generation of American thinkers. They feel that it is supported in our time by the abundant evidence of Rudolf Steiner's work. Study of this evidence deepens the world conception of Waldorf teachers, enabling them to develop a contemporary education that is profoundly sympathetic to what is central, and best, in our American cultural tradition.

Making knowledge a complete human experience.

First of all, the door is again opened to the love of nature. This is not something to be taken for granted. Strangely, the all-out pursuit of natural science in our day has not increased the love of nature. On the contrary, one observes that students of biology, chemistry, and physics can pass by the phenomena of nature with marked indifference. What Rudolf Steiner called "sub-nature"—the new kingdom of technology—interests them greatly. They study the physical effects of wind, clouds, rain, and sun; but the actual wind, clouds, rain, and sun are scarcely noticed. The same is true of their relationship to plants, birds, insects, and other creatures, during the day, and the stars, at night. Interest becomes theoretical rather than actual. If young people today are not at home in the world they live in, this is because the way of knowledge they have been given makes them casual observers of the world rather than its intimate participants in life.

---

9. "By successive states of mind all the facts of Nature are for the first time interpreted."—Ralph Waldo Emerson, *Poetry and Imagination*.

Underneath consciousness they are saying of the order of nature, as they often feel of the order of society, "I have no part in all this." But when students have been taught to feel what they are and will what they think, they are on the way to sharing the life of the universe. Young people are then at home because the phenomena of universal nature speak to what lies deepest within themselves, and they sense that somehow their own human response is of great importance to nature itself.[10]

Love of nature is the soundest guarantee that scientific interest will remain strong. Before natural science, there was natural history; and before natural history there was natural philosophy. *Philosophy* is love of knowledge. Love of the knowledge of nature was present in ancient times because people felt themselves bound to nature by a total affinity. This love has continued to support science down through succeeding ages, but now the real affinity is felt less and less. Today, science is often motivated more by the will to power than by the love of knowledge. But we may expect this substitution to be revenged, for while love brings blessing to human life in that it rightly places us close to—yet independent from—nature, the will to power alienates us from nature, yet trammels and enmeshes us within it. Nature withdraws the zest for life she could have imparted *to* one who honored her with warmth of heart in knowing; while the very "mechanisms" of nature that we human beings had thought to exploit, threaten at last to chew us up and spit us out.

The love of nature opens, in turn, the door to creative ability.

While today universal education has made almost everyone at least somewhat literate, most people know that they are not

---

10. "If you would learn the secrets of nature, you must practice more humanity than others."—Henry David Thoreau, *Journals*.

truly creative. And while we are all busy, many of our works have not benefited humanity. Often as not, we undermine ourselves by our very successes. The values we in the West bring into existence are mostly technical; and while it seems that we have created them, it might be truer to say that they have created themselves—by our hand, but often against our best interest. Too often, these values diminish the experience of being human, even as they tend to denature Nature. They are paradoxical in robbing human society at the same time they enrich it, making it the more vulnerable for their protection. In true creativeness, by contrast, it is the human being who acts; and the values brought into existence are not paradoxical. Because they issue from a balanced human experience, they actually and permanently enhance human life.

Thoughts always need a master: the thinker. When left free to follow their own promptings, every chance association begins multiplying and subdividing. They spin out forever, and their path of unwinding usually leads away from strength and away from truth. To the mere making of thoughts there is no end, perhaps no beginning, and frequently no point. This fact of experience should teach intellectuals that they are not truly being creative when they give mere mentality free rein. On the other hand, impulses and passions also have a will of their own that needs to be mastered. They, too, seek their own ends. Overly passionate and hyperactive enthusiasts are deluded when they believe they are actually in charge of their passions, and that their impulses are truly human. People find *themselves* by rightly building the bridge between thought and action. Only the thoughts that we feel and will entirely, the acts of will that we think through and completely feel, can be called our own thoughts and actions. Only in this way do we exercise proper responsibility—responsibility in the sense of contribution that returns to our lasting welfare.

The experience of knowledge, as it is striven for in Waldorf schools, brings about the rapprochement of thought and action. The result, as we have said, is a loving relationship between students and what they study. Love of the world breathes in the warmth of thoughtfulness. Out of this love springs creative power that represents world-force, yet also the humanity of the students themselves.

Creativeness is usually associated with the fine arts. Much contemporary art, however, is unworthy to be called creative, for it tends to be either a desert of abstractions, or a jungle of urgencies. It cannot be called an extension and expression of the powers that build nature, yet neither does it represent the essential human being. But when enlightened love of nature is opened up again, we may expect to see art regain its position as the healer and helper of humankind. Creative power streams ever through the universe. The right kind of knowing is a sharing in this power. When knowledge is fully experienced— above all, the knowledge of nature, in which we behold God's work of art—the same divine, creative power activates the knower right to the fingertips, producing thereby the artist, whose work will be the continuation or fulfillment of nature.

Creative ability opens the door to practical life.

The impracticality of practical minds has thus far contrived a technological civilization where it seems that the steps forward are matched by steps backward—where those who save most time by technical means actually come to have the least; where those who cover more space see less; where comforts engender dissatisfaction and restlessness; where crops grow big and nourishment shrinks; where all-purpose "progress" such as the use of atomic energy endangers the safety and health of every being on Earth. We need practicality that is practical. We need successes that really succeed. Human society today more than ever needs creative artists in the shaping of economic, political, legal, medical, agricultural, and educational affairs.

The main distinction between theoretical reformers and those who actually manage to shape events—aside from the difference in sheer energy flowing through them—is that theorists approach life from outside. They come as pious strangers, seeking to impose their good ideas on wayward reality. Those, however, who have learned to handle life as artists approach reality from within. They are at one with events. Their good ideas arise directly from the ripening of their experience of the material at hand. Their ideals are not hatched predictably out of abstract logic on the one hand, or personal ambition on the other. Rather, they are learned by such people, perhaps unexpectedly and to their surprise, as they follow the metamorphoses of real events. Such ideals appear to emerge gradually from reality itself, albeit with the help of their thought and their hands.

Why do the abstract theorists so often stumble against reality? Of theoretical minds we sense that they are too quickly finished with learning from life. They tend to work from and toward generalities that do not take full measure of actual times, places, and people. Theorists who have some success with thinking out principles often have difficulty with their application. They may not know precisely where and how to make a beginning. They may find their timing is off, that the approach offends. Theorists may eventually become discouraged from attempting to improve the recalcitrant world. All this, because the concepts of theoretical idealism tend to be drawn from the air rather than from reality. Even when a person has the facts straight and thinks true ideas, there will be trouble if reality has taught only the head. Unless knowing is an experience of the whole person, it will still not add up to "know *how*," much less to "can *do*."

Practicality opens the door to peace.

Nearly everyone wants peace today. But unless schools educate people who are practical to lead society, there is no telling whether the almost universal desire for peace will actually succeed in bringing to an end the terrible succession of wars that has thus far characterized our century.

We have repeatedly mentioned the paradoxical nature of modern technological progress. Starting from the wish to make land more fertile, we continue to reduce its natural fertility and so find ourselves chained to the necessity of ever bigger doses of fertilizer to maintain the status quo. Starting from the idea of destroying bacteria and bugs, we call into being new strains of frightening virulence. Starting from the presumably sincere wish to reduce the federal deficit, one administration after another finds itself watching this deficit grow. And starting from the desire to do something to uplift the "little people," big government shows signs that it could end by crushing them altogether.

The results of cold-blooded intelligence may seem scientific, but in practical life they will always be paradoxical, which in the end really means impractical. For every one-sidedness calls out its opposite. Cold blood calls forth hot; an overdose of rationalism calls forth an upsurge of the irrational—whether mystical, revolutionary, psychotic, or criminal. As these opposites collide inside the individual, either they engender frustration, paralysis, and atrophy; or they break out in violence and destruction. Colliding in society, they bring about stalemate—or warfare. Only a whole intelligence, maturing from complete experience, well-centered and in harmony with itself, can actually do what it sets out to do. Only such an intelligence can so master the extreme paradoxicality of modern life as to achieve real peace and real health.

An intelligence that matures from experience, that shares in the life of things, that is creative and practical, fulfills itself. It finds satisfaction in properly human pursuits. Not at war with nature or with itself, it does not project war into human society. Waldorf schools aim to develop this kind of intelligence, for in it they see the only prospect for freedom and fulfillment in the world.[11]

---

11. Appendix F contains several quotations especially relevant to this chapter.

7

Morality and the
Experience of Knowledge

The real defense of freedom is imagination, that feeling life
of the mind which actually knows because it involves itself in
its knowing, puts itself in the place where its thought goes....
The man who knows with his heart knows himself to be a
man, feels as himself, cannot be silenced. He is free no matter
where he lives. —*Archibald MacLeish*

WE HAVE TRIED TO DEMONSTRATE that real knowing,
knowing reality, can be born only of slowly maturing experience that involves the whole human being. We can further observe that any form of knowledge that fails to elicit students'
whole power of response has important consequences also for
their moral development. The more clearly we visualize all that
should enter into full-fledged cognition, the more readily can
we trace these moral consequences.

Let us imagine junior high school students who have been
brought along ever since kindergarten with the idea of looking
at the here and now in a quite factual way. Pursuing what contemporary Western education calls objective knowledge, they
try always to be logical and critical in the thoughts they think,
and very impersonal about whatever facts they are dealing
with. Their natural inclination to live into these facts, to imagine them and let their feelings work through and digest them,
has been ignored for so long that they no longer realize that
this *is* their natural inclination. What will be the effect of these
young persons' training upon their moral attitudes?

We have before us individuals who have been trained in a superficial alertness, but in a deeper unresponsiveness—souls who take a remote attitude toward both facts and thoughts. They have been trained not to involve themselves. They have no idea of being called upon either intimately or profoundly. The world passes before their eyes as a moving picture of no very great significance, as something out there that is quite unrelated to the depths of their own souls. The parade of facts passes before their outer eyes, and the "stream of consciousness," composed of miscellaneously associated ideas, passes before the inner eye. They will attach themselves strongly to neither. They will develop an indifferent attitude toward all that they come to know, and this attitude will apply to their relationship with the reality of their own soul and spirit as much as it does to their contact with other people and things.

When we follow out the results of merely educating the intellect, we shall see that a superficial response to knowledge during the school years is the beginning of what becomes moral irresponsibility later on. The "I don't care" attitude in moral questions is directly related to the "I don't care" attitude toward learning. *Moral irresponsibility* later on is a consequence of *psychological unresponsiveness* during student days. These words themselves show the connection. For one who views the world in an external or only mental way, it may seem concrete and real enough; yet it is on the way to becoming unreal. Nothing can be quite real for us that does not produce in us the personal conviction of reality. But such a conviction is the summarizing experience of our feelings and will forces, if and when these have taken part in our perceptions. A purely external world that has not been and cannot be so experienced simply does not signify for us: we feel it to be *in*significant. A world without significance, however, for all its material substantiality, is essentially unreal; and we as knowers of such a world share in its unreality; for in this kind of knowing, we are more mirrors than human beings.

Here we have the original breach of contract, the original deception. Young people are trained to say "I know" when they do not know, and they do not even suspect the existence of a difference between what they call knowing and *real knowing*. Such persons have been led by their teachers to deceive themselves as to what they truly know; and from self-deception they have not far to go before they can, with scarcely a twinge of conscience, deceive others. For an unreal student in an unreal world, plagiarism and cheating do not seem particularly important. The way is rather short from this kind of untrustworthiness in student days to misrepresentation and fraud as an adult.

Even though Shakespeare gave to a person of dubious character the words to utter, Polonius' psychology was sound when he advised: "To thine own self be true, and it must follow, as the night the day, thou canst not then be false to any man." Acquiring knowledge is the main business of education, and in our time education is the business in which young people are mainly engaged. How true to themselves are elementary and secondary students in their pursuit of knowledge?

They are scarcely true at all, since they have been educated to observe without feeling, and to arrive at externally suggested or compelled conclusions without the intuitive confirmation that should complete their experience. Thus they are without *conscience* in their knowing. "In the uttermost meaning of the words," Emerson said, "thought is devout, and devotion is thought. Deep calls unto deep." But of modern students, who follow their modern teachers, it could be more truly said: "Surface calls to surface; the world-process externally viewed calls to superficial powers of cognition. The inner humanity remains inactive and asleep; such absence makes outer human relations somewhat unreal."

Between a somewhat unreal self and a somewhat unreal world, what is more natural than an unreal relationship, one that shifts and dissolves in an ephemeral sort of way? Such a relationship is the beginning of untrustworthiness, fraud, and deception of every kind. Why do some builders, some mechanics or repairmen, some parents, and some executives of business and government on a higher level, say they have done the job, when in fact they have only gone through certain motions? These good people have no wish to do wrong. They are simply somewhat numb and uncaring toward reality. And because their bond with the real world, both outside and inside themselves, is vague, fairly minor cross-currents of fear or desire can steer them to wrongdoing. When knowledge of the world awakens only the faintest pulse of vital response in people, we cannot expect any strong bond to unite them with their responsibilities.

We have suggested that when the act of cognition leaves the deeper self untouched, both the self and the world known by that self become phantasms. But there are also other moral consequences of the too hasty, too shallow act of cognition.

It is important to notice, for instance, that the desire of the self to experience full activity of knowledge is part of an equally fundamental desire for the self to transcend itself in experience of the "other." In Emerson's words, "The one thing which we seek with insatiable desire is to forget ourselves, to be surprised out of our propriety, to lose our sempiternal memory and to do something without knowing how or why; in short to draw a new circle." Do not most of us feel cramped in our own narrowness? Are we not bored by ourselves? The I in each of us longs for release from its prison. Everyone wants to be surprised by joy. Everyone hopes to love.

Release, reinforcement, and re-creation of the I should properly come from contact with the other—such contact, for *homo sapiens* (literally, "the wise species"), is properly made through the activity of knowledge. But when knowledge is on-looking rather than in-working, there can be no flowing of the self into another, or of the other into the self. The self must then look for a different way out of its solitary confinement. And today this is the beginning of a whole new category of immoral tendencies and actions. The desire for stimulation that ends in drug addiction, eroticism, violence, and so on may be traced back to the simple, central fact that knowledge has lost its savor, its ability to touch and stimulate human beings. The savor of knowledge depends upon the degree to which the self shares in the actual life of what surrounds it: becomes as strong as granite, as humble as water, as joyful as air, in the participatory knowing of these aspects of nature.

The self *will* out. Drugs, sex, speed, and rebellion seem to offer ways out, but the trouble with all of these is that their ways are illusory. At the end of each adventure lies not freedom but chains. The sensual thrill leaves sensibility deadened; one's forcible outburst weakens.

True knowing, deeper knowing, intuitive-participatory knowing is the proper thrill and the right way "out" for the human spirit. It is Emerson's "true nectar, which is the ravishment of the intellect by coming nearer to the fact." This sacred act of knowledge lifts what would have been only sensory experience to the level of the spirit. Sensory experiences that bypass the human spirit degenerate into immoral appetites; they pull people down. But when the same sensations and perceptions awaken the answering human spirit, their thrill is the very essence of joyful living.

Humanity is replenished through love. What people love, that they have. When we love the environment we live in, the people we meet, the work we do, the world fills us with its own positive content. We grow generous and charitable.

Our overflowing goodwill is felt by others as a blessing, which they gladly return in their goodwill toward us.

But those who do not love, do not have this ever-renewed fullness. They are like the well in which water not only fails to overflow as a spring, but in which the water level is progressively dropping. Because they look upon the world around themselves from a distance, with indifference or distaste, they find nothing in it to touch their hearts. For such people, events do not yield their secret life. They are all masked. Masks cannot be loved. When love fails, the wellspring of the affirming self sinks. The receding waters create a kind of suction that we may call negative selfhood, or selfishness. The self does not flow outwards into life, but seeks to draw life in toward itself. It tries to fill its lack of *being* by much *having*. And this is a chief characteristic of modern Western humanity. We have an addiction to possessions. Happiness is sought primarily through the quest for money, power, and prestige.

The difficulty is, a dying spring cannot be replenished by pouring more water into it, but only by a self-renewed up-welling from its own depths. No amount of desire to *possess* things can make up for the failure to *love* things. "What a man loves, that he has; but by desire he robs himself of that love." Desire *is* selfishness; its suction comes from inner emptiness. This emptiness is a state of non-being. Non-being is a hunger that asks to be fed. The only food that would genuinely still the hunger of non-being is being. But our culture, instead of recognizing what is wrong and learning how to remedy it, has hastened still further along the road that brought it in the first place to hunger instead of satisfaction. It pursues its insatiable appetite for material goods and services with a drive that threatens to devastate the entire Earth.

Who does not love, cannot create. And the one who can neither love nor create is no real human being. To become creative one must know how to rise above personal limits and take inspiration from the other and the higher. And then one must know how to find the way back, allowing this inspiration to flow through oneself into deeds of initiation. To bring power from *beyond* the self *into* the self, that it may flow *out* again through loving acts, is to become creative. This is the gain of right cognition, and the loss to be expected from wrong cognition.

"The man who can enter and leave at will is at home," said George Macdonald. Through right cognition we find the way out of ourselves lovingly, and back into ourselves creatively; and thus we make ourselves at home, yet free, in the universe.

PART THREE

8

Genius as the Goal
of Education

As the whole has its law, so each individual has his genius.
. . . the true romance which the world exists to realize will be
the transformation of genius into practical power.

—*Emerson*

IT IS GENERALLY assumed that while every child possesses some talent, genius can be ascribed to very few. For this reason, the development of talent rather than of genius has become the goal of education. I should like to suggest that we are reversing the true order of things, turning them upside down, to the harm of society as well as of the individual.

In the original sense of the word, genius is a guiding, inspiring principle that is accessible, if we will, to every human being. This source of strength and guidance is not concerned with special abilities but with the whole person. It can use whatever talents an individual has. An education works either to close or to open the channel between children and their genius.

Each human being has talent by the mere fact of having been born as male or female, of this inheritance or that. But such talent always tends toward bias, toward one-sidedness: by having this, one does not have that; and in simply following one's bent, one does not necessarily contribute to the common good. It is genius that transforms a mere mixture of specialized abilities into a true compound, a whole personality. It is genius that holds individual striving to the common good.

If we compare health with height in children, we have no difficulty observing that more children are healthy than are tall. Obviously, too, health is more important than being tall. The comparison has implications for schooling: more can be done to help a child acquire health than height. Yet American schools, the innovative as well as the traditional, have been moving steadily away from the purpose of healing, harmonizing, and humanizing their students in an inwardly healthy way. Most are plainly bent on talent. Of course, the talents that count above all others in the school years are verbal and mathematical facility, a retentive memory, and the power of logical analysis, as these are measured by IQ tests.

In our time, school is the gateway for all children to the whole of life, yet the criterion of a school's favor is nothing so universal as humanity and the love of humanity, or capacity to be grateful to life and enjoy it, or will to contribute. It is not courage, reverence, integrity, or goodwill. All of these are central qualities of moral health that, as we shall see, lie near to genius. Yet at present the criterion determining favor in schools is primarily aptitude for school work. School tasks use portions of the mind that are relatively unimportant for genius, yet society accords elite standing to the scholars in whom these kinds of mentality stand out. Such "gifted" individuals come to expect, and are generally expected by society, to take positions of leadership later on—not only in higher education, but in business, government, and the professions. More and more, it would seem, schools are expecting talent to take charge of our civilization.

For the idea of genius to be forgotten is bad enough; it is worse to have it replaced by something almost opposite. That just this substitution has taken place is evident from the fact that genius is now popularly regarded as talent-in-the-highest-degree: a peculiarly intense form of specialized ability! The child who at five can perform mental operations that are commonplace among ten year-olds is accorded the standing of "genius." But often such genius betokens simply that one is getting prematurely old, that one is suffering from hypertrophy of certain aspects of the brain. Plainly looked at, it may remind us of a sickness.

One who starts from the idea of inspired human soundness contained in the ancient idea of genius, and then watches what is going on in modern high schools and even elementary schools will have good reason to be troubled. One sees students who are unsound, ill-balanced, perhaps even immoral, yet who show early brightness and are given preferential treatment—an "enriched" curriculum, extra-capable teachers, and so on—while the sometimes sounder but not so bright are gathered into second-, third-, and fourth-rate groups that are educated with less hope and less care. While the technical advantages of this kind of grouping under certain circumstances are not to be denied, the human consequences, for the fast as well as the slow students—and for the future of society—may prove very harmful.

It is bad for possessors of a limited talent like academic brightness to think of themselves, and be thought of, as humanly superior. It is wrong for them to be encouraged to accentuate even further a relatively technical ability that already thrives at the expense of their humanity as a whole. And it is equally unfortunate that those who learn more slowly—because their very real, very important gifts are of heart and will rather than head—should think of themselves as unworthy and become habituated to the sense of failure. Often they are simply not yet ready to perform academic tasks. The response of most schools, however, is to drill unready children in just the intellectual capacities they do not yet possess, while aptitudes of greater moral and social significance that they often do possess, go unrecognized and undeveloped. Frequently these hidden powers lie closer to the genius that teaches human beings how to be human than does intellectuality; for while intellect *that has overcome itself* may be the glory of humankind, complacency about intellect as a talent is perhaps the greatest single obstacle in the modern age to the higher inspiration and guidance people need, and have the right to hope for, from their genius.

> Thy Daemon, that's thy spirit which keeps thee. . . .
> —Shakespeare, *Antony and Cleopatra*

The idea of genius has come to us from ancient times. What did it signify to the Greeks, Romans, and other earlier peoples?

Genius was once an intuitively perceived reality: the protective and guiding spirit that gave each person prepared to receive it the wisdom, or love, or power needed for good deeds on Earth. A person's genius was a higher self that could be called upon to infuse life with values transcending personal limits. "Genius," says the *Oxford Universal Dictionary,* stating the ancient view, "is a tutelary god or attendant spirit allotted to every person at birth to preside over destiny in life."

Heraclitus, speaking for the mystery wisdom of Greece, said: "Genius is a deity." Socrates called this deity his daemon. He tried always to obey it, finding that he made mistakes only when he failed to heed its prompting.

> You have heard me speak at sundry times and in divers places of an oracle or sign that comes to me, and is the divinity that Meletus ridicules in the indictment. This sign, which is a kind of voice, first began to come to me when I was a child; it always forbids but never commands me to do anything that I am going to do.

Plutarch says somewhere that a person's daemon or genius can be seen by initiates as hovering above the head like a star. Wordsworth was doubtless referring to this tradition in his famous Ode:

> Our birth is but a sleep and a forgetting:
> The soul that rises with us, our life's Star,
> Hath elsewhere had its setting,
> And cometh from afar.

The French word for genius is *genie.* This is close to *jinni,* the Arabic word for an inspiring spirit. In Hebrew and Christian theology, however, the intermediaries between God and humanity, and closest to human beings, have been called guardian angels. According to Genesis, God created humanity in His own image, a little lower than the angels. The task of angels is to mediate divine wisdom, love, and power to us, each of us being attended by our own inspiring guide.

The similarity among these Greek, Roman, Arabian, and Hebrew views of genius is much greater than their difference. For all these peoples, genius was the norm, as well as the crown, of full human development. Genius was the spiritual possibility of *every* human being. It was not, however, a natural endowment but a supernatural grace, and in this respect above all it differed radically from mere talent, even the greatest talent.

Thus for ancient humanity, genius was an agency of the divine spirit that descended from above; while for modern humanity genius is no more than a name for earthly talent raised to its highest degree.

How, in ancient times, did people prepare themselves so that genius might work in them? First of all, by their confidence in the existence of higher orders of being than themselves; by their sense that the better part of human nature was to be sought in this higher order; and by their understanding of earthly life as a mystery woven of super-earthly forces, and therefore manageable only by such forces.

Thus there were preparatory conditions. The seeker of genius must develop obedience, for example, and humility. Ambition, pride, and self-will cut the soul off from its divine source. Fear and desire distort inspiration, when they do not foreclose it altogether. The sacred water can spring up only in a pure cup, and the bolt of sacred power can be endured only by an upright and steady heart.

The pagan idea of immortal genius and the Christian idea of divine grace are very closely related. Both acknowledge: "It is the Lord that doeth the work." Both seek perfection of the earthly vessel so that what is higher may enter into it as fully as possible. And both conceive the road to this perfection in similar ways, essential being the overcoming of disharmony and imbalance. Despite certain differences, the Christian saint and the pagan hero are much alike. Equally they are people of genius: equally they act under grace for the benefit of humanity.

The ancient view—which actually lasted until the last hundred years or so, particularly among artists and philosophers of the Romantic or Transcendental streams—admitted that not many would establish a working relationship with their genius. Not many would achieve results so outwardly marked that history could record them. But at the same time, neither was genius thought to be reserved for the few. It hovered over all; when not near, then far; but always there. And genius was not "possessed" by any person; rather, it possessed the person. It had little to do, specifically, with intellect as such, but much to do with the heart and will. Its working depended more upon the character one might aspire to develop than upon the abilities one was endowed with by birth. Indeed, it withdrew from those who were pleased with their own earthly endowment, while it approached those who, while knowing how inadequate their own faculties were, continued with God-given compassion and valor to do what they could for others.

In ancient times, as pagan genius became Christian grace, one realized more and more clearly that divine sanction would no more be withheld from a soul who sought it humbly for the sake of service, than human assistance would be withheld by an earthly father from his willing and helpful child. Christians remembered Christ's words: "Whatsoever ye shall ask in my name, that will I do." In this sense, Christ was looked to as the Genius of geniuses: the Genius of the whole of humankind.

Man's health and greatness consist in his being a channel through which heaven flows to Earth. —*Emerson*

Does it really make much difference whether genius is regarded as inspiration that approaches the harmonious and dedicated from above, as a visitation of grace, or whether it is some highly perfected ability that belongs to persons simply by reason of the constitution with which they were born? *If* the quality of education deriving from the two views were about the same, one would be impatient of attempts to debate such a question. But it is not the same. Experience shows that the two conceptions of genius make a radical difference. The consequences that follow upon whether a method of education adopts the one or the other as its criterion of excellence are as far apart as reality and illusion, or as wholesome gladness and sick sorrow.

Much that we associate with the traditions of liberal or humanistic education once had the goal of teaching students that there *is* a heaven, that it *can* flow to Earth through humanity, and that every individual should desire to establish this flow— as the first and last condition of human well-being; indeed, as one's duty toward the rest of creation. Such was the teaching of the most ancient Mysteries; such was still being taught in dilute form, until recently, even among the most rationalistic Western nations. This tradition carries on the original doctrine of genius. Wherever it has been lost, education as a liberating and truly humane discipline has also been lost.

The heaven that flows through humanity was conceived not as something foreign, but as the better part of human individuality. Essentially, human beings are born of the spirit, and at death return to the spirit. During earthly life in a physical body, one made the fullest use of earthly brain and muscle; but the essential in one's being remained transcendent. Every person's true self *continued* to participate in the divine world. To make of the lower self a channel through which this heaven might flow into Earth existence was therefore to overcome the illusions of competence conjured by the body, and to lie low in the power of the Lord.

To strengthen the link between bodily self and spiritual self—between the local person and what Emerson called the Over-soul—truly liberal forms of education have always imposed moral discipline. Discipline is, of course, necessary if the lesser is to be made worthy of the greater. But the perfection of discipline lies in self-discipline. Since every discipline calls for discipleship, in the case of self-discipline we may ask: discipleship to whom? Can the blind lead the blind? There must be a self, a self of one's own, who is not blind. This Self is one's genius. *Self*-discipline is impossible to conceive in any real sense without the idea of genius.

Given the focus of modern attitudes upon the advancement of talent and ego in the lower sense, there is little background of expectation or justification nowadays for a school's effort to maintain moral discipline in its student body. High school students reject guidance from their elders, yet they have no idea of how or where to look for either the guidance or the strength required to discipline themselves. Without access to the kind of strength that is invulnerable, students fall victim to many kinds of fear. Without the hope of serving as a vessel for spiritual energies greater than themselves, students are helpless before their own desires. They have no incentive to make themselves worthy. Worthy of what?

> The purest efforts of will of which we are capable cannot lift us up even to the abstaining from wrong to our neighbor. In order to fulfil the commonest law . . . we must rise into a loftier region altogether, a region that is above law, because it is spirit and life that make the law.
>
> —George Macdonald

Because we have lost touch with the idea that strength from above can be added to our human striving, a large portion of Western humankind today feels confused, unhappy, and basically helpless The trials of our time, in that they demand more than natural talents can deliver, could be for each of us the very opportunity to rise to a higher level: to call upon our supernatural self, our genius. But due to the failure of nerve that results from materialistic education, what might have been the lift that answers a hard challenge becomes the put-down of hopelessness.

Life these days is doubtful as to its meaning, difficult as to its living. As we laypeople begin to see that neither scientists nor statesmen, neither preachers nor teachers, have the saving clue, we feel thrown back upon ourselves. We can become fatally discouraged when we think of pitting our own slender strength against problems that experts of great talent and high position have found impossible, even though these problems, as they affect us personally, are of course much scaled down. Unless we recall that "Genius is the ability to do the impossible," and know that genius can be ours as well as someone else's, we are hardly persuaded to accept our full measure of responsibility for the state of the world or to do our utmost to insure change.

If "ordinary" people are to gain insight, feel courage, assume control, and thus find the happiness that seems so elusive, they will have to convince themselves that something in themselves is of immeasurable significance and has unlimited capacity for bringing about the good. They can then understand why the paradoxes of progress in modern society *must* become more and more outrageous until we all begin to make the free choice to live from this higher source within ourselves. We are being taught by events that it takes genius simply to live ordinary life well.

None are so poorly endowed that they cannot achieve the good they truly want, if they will just acknowledge and invite the higher self to overshadow life. For genius working through the mind will bring wisdom, genuine intelligence as needed for practical life; genius working through the heart will bring the gift of love; and genius, working through the will, will bring success to simple endeavors that experts can only wonder at.

If the natural mind is clever, it can wrest from experience certain kinds of knowledge. It cannot, however, discover the value and purpose of life. To pull the sword of *meaning* from the rock of external appearance requires more than subtlety, more than power.

Again, if the natural faculties of enjoyment are healthy, life may afford many pleasures. But none of these pleasures will quite awaken love. To fail in love, especially the love of other human beings, is to become profoundly neurotic. Everywhere in the modern world people are starved for love. They are disheartened that love does not come toward them, to give them joy. And so they go seeking. But when love does not stream toward us, it is because it does not stream out of us. To be loved, one must love. And truly to love is possible only for one who has been made abundant and generous by coming into touch with the divine ground of being.

If, finally, human nature has strength and skill, it may accomplish feats of power, perhaps with great finesse. But ultimately these feats will be defeated. For all one's resourcefulness, the natural person is absolutely helpless against the attacks of adverse fate and the finality of death. Mortal talent can neither understand nor master the destiny that rules these events, for they concern the immortal nature of humanity.

In reality, we do not have the option of whether we shall draw toward the realm of genius or remain stuck in our natural selves. There is essentially no such thing as a natural human self. We are constituted natural/supernatural. The sense of selfhood that we have in ordinary life is not something that can stand alone. Not really a thing in itself, it is more like the flame of a candle as seen in a mirror. The mirror-flame could not survive removal of the true flame; no more can natural selfhood, with its several talents, prosper when the supernatural self is ignored. We do not really have the choice of whether we shall seek wisdom, or content ourselves with knowledge; seek love and joy, or content ourselves with pleasures; seek creative inspiration, or just plod along like ordinary people.

Contemporary humanity imagines that the will to knowledge and the capacity for knowledge may be taken for granted; but we have these only because we follow from the ancients, for whom the roots of the tree of knowledge were planted deep in religious experience. Religion is born of reverence and awe. Then religious experience was still first-hand, its power to nourish philosophy was great: the whole human being was enlisted. In our time, however, the power of philosophy is not the kind that is born of whole-souled wonder; and the power of recent forms of science to *continue* the quest for knowledge concerning the questions that really interest the human soul is proving to be least of all. The motives of science today are largely economic. To hold interest in the pursuit of knowledge one can of course take further steps into economic technology, as we have long been doing. But this is already to abandon any *heart-felt* desire to know. The technology that harnesses nature for physical benefit is certainly important; but it does not answer questions that matter to the human soul and spirit. Thus while one can speak of wisdom as the fruit of the tree of knowledge, it is even truer to say that knowledge is a fruit borne by the tree of wisdom. Unless the wisdom-sap keeps running, we shall not long continue to pick sound fruit of knowledge.

What is true of the generic relationship between wisdom and knowledge is equally true of that between love and pleasure. Love is the mother; pleasure, the legitimate offspring. A human being filled with love finds inexhaustible pleasure in his contacts with the world. Because love flows through his experiences, transient pleasures become lasting joys. But when we forget eternal being and can therefore no longer find lasting signifi-cance in the changing world, true love becomes impossible. When love withdraws, pleasures, far from enhancing life, be-come parasitical upon it. Pleasure is no more able to sustain it-self on the level of purely natural existence than is knowledge. Sensual pleasures are self-devouring. Unless the experience of pleasure is turned outward, unless it confers the supernatural gift of love upon its object, pleasure will become suffering. In the vain effort to maintain vividness, it will exploit both the self and the other. Signs that this is what is happening in Western culture today are everywhere at hand. Both the human body and the body of Earth are being exhausted in the pursuit of plea-sures that grow ever more elusive.

What, finally, is the relationship between creative inspira-tion and the capacity to do ordinary work? How long can earthly talents carry on earthly work for earthly goals without the intervention of the transcendent factors we have been grouping under the name of genius?

One way to look at the matter, of course, is to believe that the healthy human organism can certainly perform work according to its ability, essential to its health being only good food, proper rest, control of disease, and so on. One may, however, without going into details, ask whether, even as there is something in all of us that transcends our physical organisms, there are not also transcendent forces that play into all the earthly conditions that support the organism?

Food, for example, is a cosmic as well as an earthly reality. Jung said that for him plants always seemed "the thoughts of God." Because humankind once looked upon the whole of nature in this way, the saying of grace before meals used to be a universal custom. People thanked God for the gift of Nature; in partaking of Nature's bounty they felt that more than bodily powers entered them. But now that we regard air, water, earth, and the produce of Earth as purely physical resources, negative consequences for the health and strength of our civilization are becoming obvious. Even while we place great emphasis upon the conditions of health, we sap the energy men and women need in order to be fully active, by all the ways in which we erode the fertility of Earth and reduce the nutritive content of foods. Degenerative diseases of many kinds, taking an immense toll in working days wasted, indicate the depletion of life-force in especially those nations that imagine their cleverness is on the point of gaining control over nature.

The same dependence of the lesser reality upon the greater is evident in the case of proper rest. Proper rest means chiefly sleep. Sleep is certainly of the utmost importance for work. But what is sleep, and what makes sleep refreshing? Ancient world conceptions agreed that in sleep the individual is released from particularity in order to be restored and inspired by the universal. He leaves the drought and dust of physical existence, to bathe in living waters. But in modern times, sleep has been robbed of its high mystery; it is no longer prepared for as a holy event. Nowadays, people lie down but cannot sleep; sleep, but are not restored. They are irritable and anxious, day after day. To meet the need of humankind, billions of tranquilizers for the day and sleeping pills for the night are brought forward. But the result of these is no influx of vital energy or uplift by creative inspiration.

The power to work in a practical way on the most ordinary problems in the outer world rests at last upon strengths of body and soul. The former derive from food properly grown and respected, and from sleep rightly valued and prepared. Both food and sleep are important also for the soul, since it is hard for a sound mind to work through an unsound body. The vital energy of food and the creative inspiration of sleep, necessary for health of body and soul, indispensable for everyday work, both enter earthly existence from a higher realm.

If we all lived up to the promises of our infancies, we should all be geniuses. —*Schiller*

Many things can cut a person off from the flow of heavenly power. In the foregoing essays we have drawn special attention to a kind of *blockage* that should be the particular concern of educators—specifically, premature and predominating intellectuality. "Pure intellect is the pure devil," said Emerson. As Plato showed in his parable of the cave, the world of intellect is a world of shadows. Its mirror-play converts spiritual reality, whether outside or inside us, into images that copy life but are not alive. The spiritual that is the open secret of our earthly existence is therefore a nothing to the intellectualist who is honest about experience. For such a person the world is physically substantial but spiritually meaningless—a body uninhabited. In this mirror world, the unimportant is taken for real and the important for unreal; all things are moved, but nowhere is there a mover. In this world God is truly dead.

Our argument throughout this book has been that intellectual cognition should appear in the soul of the young human being *after* he or she has completed earlier stages in which feeling and will are established. When the right time comes, intellect appears very naturally. A normal further evolution of the modern soul leads it to see that the conditions of our beleaguered yet promising time, conditions both outer and inner, call upon intellect to grow above itself, to become more intuitive and creative than it now is. But schools today are interfering most destructively with this evolution. In bringing youth to intellectuality too soon and too insistently, they are paralyzing the forces that in due course should lead beyond intellectuality. Failing to recognize the very different forms cognition should take in the earlier stages of child development, they also block the higher forms of cognition that those in maturity today would otherwise naturally be seeking.

Without doubt, the secret of genius is the secret of earliest childhood. Traherne, Blake, Wordsworth, Masefield, Thoreau, and many other poets have testified out of their own experience that the link between the eternal and the temporal self, as also consciousness of the spiritual background of the nature we see around us, is strongest in early childhood. "Except ye become again as little children, ye shall not see the kingdom of Heaven." The creative human archetype most fills us when our mortal clay is still plastic. Steiner said that the works done by children before the age of three—in fashioning their bodies, in achieving erect posture, and in mastering speech—are greater deeds than any they will accomplish later. They are done by the higher being in children before they begin to recapitulate humanity's fall—that is, before self-consciousness appears and they come to address themselves as I. "Infancy," said Emerson, "is the perpetual Messiah, which comes into the arms of fallen men, and pleads with them to return to paradise"—that is, to regain unity with the larger I, "the Light that lighteth every man that cometh into the world."

In the last analysis, behind all the vices and mistakes that break our ties with the higher self, is egoism. The fearful, hyperactive, intensely competitive modern world almost compels people to build upon egoism. The world trades in talent; talents compete for the center of the stage; and too often the success of one person of talent spells failure for another. While there may be a viewpoint that can survey the whole scene in such a way as to show that justice is always done at last, and that destiny is ultimately fair as well as sure, to reach this view one must be lifted to higher ground than that upon which talent stands. One must be able to hope as much for others' aims as for one's own; and as to which shall prevail, one must be content to let divine wisdom decide.

But such an attitude is impossible for the lower self, which must always consider itself the center of value. The ego is forever striving to rearrange events so as to place itself in this center, and it therefore finds itself at odds with all other egos engaged in the same enterprise. To come free from ego-competition, which our present education tends so markedly to encourage, requires that one feel centered in the world-process as a whole. This feeling, very young children coming freshly into this world from a higher one, obviously have. They share unselfconsciously in every value they encounter, before personal egoism has developed in them to the point where they would like to put their own value first.

Children start out with a sense for the universal. To many parents this fact is uncomfortable, for it gives the child a certain remoteness—from which he or she must be called back by stimulation—tickling and chucking under the chin. Teachers, too, find the universality of children uncomfortable. To them it may appear as a baffling incomprehension of the importance of school success. But actually many a child's unwillingness to condense into ego-status in the classroom is a positive rather than a negative trait. It shows that genius has not yet left the child, who is still vitally related to the whole.

The child *should* be father to the woman and the man. Happy the person who can retain the youthful spirit of genius into later years. In maturity, we should all draw strength from our youth as mid-day draws from morning—and as morning, in turn, draws from the foregoing night. At mid-day, we shall be best able to write the morning's music down, if we remember that the song was already there when day dawned.

Let us, as parents and educators, behold earliest childhood with the prayer that our eyes may be more open to its mysteries. May we learn from the child the secret of human genius. Boredom, cynicism, and exhaustion await the culture whose schools prefer bright little old people to genuine children. Real children are often too full of action and feeling to score well in tests of intellect; their embracing sympathies may show up in the classroom as lack of attention; their imaginative flights may seem factual foolishness. Yet the real child is one of God's fools. Teachers do well who seek in this folly the beginning of wisdom.

9

Authority, Discipline, and Freedom

Who has more obedience than I masters me, though he should not raise his finger. Round him I must revolve by the gravitation of spirits. —*Emerson*

THOSE WHO DISPUTE about how to educate free individualities must debate the effects of childish obedience upon adult self-reliance, of unquestioning trust and belief in authority during the first school years that lead to the critical thinking that enables a mature individual later on to steer clear of illusions. One party will hold that if the goal of education is an eventual power to judge, make choices, and summon initiative, these practices should begin at once; for only practice makes perfect. Children should be left to draw upon their own resources as soon and as far as possible. Parents and teachers should, as it were, make themselves small so as not to place their children at a disadvantage. They should be sparing of example, and minimize their authority, speaking when spoken to, advising when asked for advice.

The other party to the dispute about how to educate sturdy individuals usually holds that young children are not ready for freedom. They will come into their own soon enough; but in the meantime, as preparation, they should bow to authority, believe in their betters, and undergo discipline. The goal is freedom, but freedom must be deserved. As the "school of hard knocks" prepares a person to value and use well the conditions of ease, and as deprivation is the best training for affluence, so the youngster should be taught to receive humbly the judgment of his elders before getting any idea of putting forward opinions. Young people should certainly follow before they attempt to lead.

A sound idea of the relationship between freedom and discipline-under-authority combines these more usual concepts. On the one hand, it is obviously unfair and inefficient to expect of children what they are not ready to do. They do not start out with judgment and power of decision. They have no self-knowledge, and are reluctant even to be self-aware. To treat them as if they were able, or wanted, to think things through raises in one part of their being an empty self-importance. In a deeper, truer part, it makes them feel bewildered and unhappy. Obviously, the pupil must go through the stages of apprenticeship before he can be accorded the status of a master. All this is clear. On the other hand, to whom shall the girl or boy be apprenticed if not precisely to a master; and of what will the apprenticeship consist, if not learning the actual steps in the real craft? These steps advance on the straight way that leads to the goal, related to it not indirectly but directly.

Before we go on, however, to consider the stages through which every young person passes on the way to full powers, let us pause briefly to make the special connection between this subject and the epistemological theme of the present book. The difference between theories of the relationship between authority and freedom can always be shown to rest upon different theories of knowledge, which derive from different conceptions of what is basic in human nature.

Those who think primarily along biological lines will tend to locate a person's individuality in the physical body, picturing the child to be educated as a small being who contains inherent abilities and is moved to use these abilities. This small one is loomed over by adults who are full of themselves, who have their own abilities and life-habits, but who, being larger and stronger than the child, wield "authority." These adults favor their own preferences over the child's. They impose their thoughts and ways of doing things upon children before these have had a chance to bring forth their own first responses to life. Such adults, by their demands for attention and obedience, suppress in children what is most valuable, what is unique and individual.

An educator who starts from trans-biological, idealistic assumptions, however, looks away from the small organism that is striving to grow larger. Attention is fixed upon something very great that is striving, as it were, to grow smaller: something striving to enter into and work out from the small physical body. This larger self is at one with universal reason, with the "oversoul." It is truth, and the same for all; yet it is also the essence of every particular individuality. The educator knows that this great light can shine into and through the small vessel only to the extent that the latter is made pliant, receptive, and transparent. In this task teachers find their vocation. They do not apologize for their authority, because they feel that when through the *art* of teaching with love they can induce their small charges to welcome strong guidance, they have actually opened them to their own higher possibilities.

A lenient, permissive strategy seeks to interfere with the organism as little as possible, assuming that it is most itself and freest when it can live out in-built aptitudes and drives. The sterner disciplinary strategy, by contrast, finds individuality in something above and beyond the organism. It knows that when young people are willing, because of love, to side with the teacher against themselves, they gain the upper hand over their own organisms, which represent much of what is *not* individual in them.

Those who observe that objective truth impresses itself upon the thinking organism will see the need for obedience to authority during the learning process. They will understand how obedience actually gives mastery, even as humility raises up and empowers. Anyone, however, who supposes that organisms are themselves capable of thinking, does not really believe in objective truth. This view will tend to shrink from discipline, as though it were a form of bullying. For if we think "truth" is largely subjective, every individuality having its own truth, we will picture those persons as freest who from childhood have been most allowed to conceive and deal with things in their own way.

After our discussion of genius, it should be abundantly clear that in our view people are happiest when they can identify themselves with something they feel to be superior, something they can admire and love wholeheartedly. Individual human beings feel raised and fulfilled rather than belittled or suppressed by their reverence for values higher than themselves. And children's faithful obedience to a will that they acknowledge to be above them does more for their lasting *self*-assurance than any amount of praise and encouragement to proceed according to their own ideas. Human beings pass through many stages in development, and each stage should be handled somewhat differently from the others; but there is no time when the human soul really wants to turn in upon itself. Its deepest longing is always to open outwards to what lies beyond itself, and to offer this greater reality whichever of its capacities is at the moment most precious and central. A sound theory of education for freedom and individuality, therefore, will try to identify the normal stages of child development and ask itself two questions concerning each stage: a) toward what shall the child turn? and b) what form will the child's love take?

Let me attempt to indicate the natural stages through which every human being passes on the way to freedom. My particular concern will be to show that children's imitativeness, trust, and obedience are neither postponements of freedom nor probationary trials preceding it. They are themselves the very stuff of freedom. They are the forms the integral quest for freedom takes in childhood and youth.

Strange as it may seem, the authority of the adults in children's lives is the very prototype of the creative individuality, the authorship, to which they aspire. The quality of their present authority will have much to do with the quality of their future freedom. To be an authority is to author and to authorize: it is power of initiative and burden of responsibility. That child is most likely to become creative and responsible, who has been educated through full respect for authority.

For children, authority is found first of all in adults. This authority is to them what sunshine is to plants. It is their life-giving inspiration, the necessary condition of their upward growth toward eventual blossoming and bearing fruit. Preschool children turn to the example of the adults who care for them. That example is for them an absolute. Altogether naturally, they give themselves to it. The model may not be a good one, but their unconditional openness to it, their immediate and complete imitation of it, are good. Indeed, they are the only traits that will permit them to accomplish the great things they must accomplish in the first years of life. How very much infants have to learn can be appreciated from the task that confronts them when they are to take possession of the abstruse complexities of inflected speech. They are only attentive for a short time—absorbent, and adaptive enough to conform themselves perfectly to spoken language. Could they during this stage separate themselves from their environment in critical independence, they would no longer be modifiable to the depth, or with the speed and subtlety, required for mastery of their native tongue. Their valuable plasticity will only be hardened by premature use of the critical mind. Functionally, they will tend to become somewhat number and dumber. The "behavioral modification" that children's organisms need to undergo would not take place. We must admit that it were far better for them to imitate faithfully the example of bad speech than to lose the miraculous power of imitation itself, for this is the only way to master good speech.

As we have observed in Chapter 5, the youngest children bring to the adult world, for its shaping influence, first of all their propensity to act, to *do*. Adult example stimulates and formulates this will-to-do. Children in the middle years of elementary school, by contrast, offer their teachers something new: their capacity for feeling. Being already less extroverted than at first, they respond to adult authority now in a more inward way: through wonder, trust, and belief. Could they not believe wholeheartedly in their parents and teachers, their intimate life-processes would be withdrawn from the kind of education that they have only these few years to gain. Their souls would harden; the drama of the world could no longer move them in their depths, nor could it articulate them all the way into their extremities. Their souls would become somewhat ineducable.

The unquestioning trust of children in those who are responsible for their education is precisely the quality that opens them also to the educative effect of the rest of the world. If they close themselves against their teachers, they will tend to be closed to all else. Those who suppose that children of eight or ten can be fully responsive to their parents but critical of their teachers— or vice versa—are mistaken. A withdrawal from any weakens the bond with all. Far better that children of this age should trust what in some respects is not worthy of trust than that their whole capacity to draw sunlight into their souls be darkened. Misguided teachers who refuse to let children trust them implicitly, teachers who will not stand firm and let the sun of "right feeling" shine through them upon children, are subtracters of light. Their mistaken zeal to stimulate critical independence at this stage is felt by elementary school children themselves as burdensome rather than liberating. It introduces a blighting chill where all should be warmth and growth.

We come now to adolescence. Adolescent youths are happiest when they can find a hero or heroine upon whom to model their striving. Even at this stage, when in normal development critical thinking has begun to press legitimate claims, an ardent love for ideal figures, a heartfelt discipleship, are still of greatest importance. The ability to admire, the willingness to obey, bring to perfection all the latent powers of thinking, feeling, and will; and the capacity of a young man or woman to emulate is so great a virtue that it makes up for any deficiencies skeptics might presume to find in the object of admiration. Doubtless, the young disciple sees something in a hero that the onlooker does not see, something that is worthy.

Adolescence has no less need for trust and obedience than has infancy, but the nature of the authority to which adolescence turns has changed. Authority moves gradually during these years from persons to the impersonal, from the human level to the ideal. The critical judgment now coming to the fore justifiably examines *persons* in the light of *ideas*. What is intrinsically—that is, ideally—true and good becomes the standard of judgment. This transition from human authority to spiritual authority means that things are no longer so because the parent or teacher says they are so. They must be scrutinized in the light of the older students' own thoughts. And their thoughts are not without light, for by the end of high school it has in fact begun to have intimations of the ultimate source of light that was always there behind every person whom they previously had looked to as "light-givers." At this stage they are ready to pass from true persons to truth as such.

Two things are particularly hard to understand for many people today. The first riddle is how a youth who in childhood looked up uncritically to teachers, at first imitating them, then believing in them to the fullest extent, can be expected at sixteen or twenty to form truly independent judgments. The second is how, if the responsible adults really wish this young person to be free to arrive at life's answers independently, they can feel justified in continuing to exercise authority over the young person's behavior all the way up until she or he leaves home and school for good. The misunderstanding in both cases arises from a tendency to reason according to the logic of abstract words rather than according to the reality of actual cases.

Many suppose that if children have been formed in their bodily habits through imitation of adults, and in their feeling-life through trust, belief, and love, when they come to the time for having their own thoughts, they will take shape altogether predictably; for such individuals will then simply express as concepts the dispositions of habit and feeling previously acquired. The young adult will lack the basis for independent judgment, for "As the twig is bent, so grows the tree." Those who think in this way will obviously want to minimize the influence they exert upon the behavior and feelings of the earlier stages of children's development. And if nevertheless they must take charge at times during these years, they will *as soon as possible* (during high school and even junior high) abdicate their real control over behavior, resigning themselves to fond hope and occasional exhortation. In the name of strengthening young people in their own judgment and control, but more actually perhaps out of fear or lack of love, they will continue to house, feed, and finance them, whatever their actions.

The fact is that children can be taught through deeds, and then through feelings, without being in any way indoctrinated. This fact is overlooked by advocates of freedom who will *reason* interminably with them on every subject at any stage. Such people fail to provide substance for the heart and will of children, but they do not hesitate to work upon their minds—which is what they presumably most wanted to keep free. For children, the result of such "reasonings" is a weariness in body and soul, a head full of already formulated concepts—and perhaps an abiding distaste for rationality in general. This kind of result is avoided when teachers guide the children's feelings about the beautiful and ugly, the noble and ignoble, in a purely artistic way, avoiding many rational "evaluations" and definitions of just what shall be considered beautiful or ugly, noble or ignoble and why. Children so guided will be entirely able, when middle adolescence comes, to think their own thoughts; for the conceptual world will have remained, as it were, virgin territory for them. At the right moment, they enter it, look about, and make their own discoveries, with the very same joy felt by the explorer of a new continent. They know that every insight they come to is their own; and it can easily happen that their insights will be a great surprise, even incomprehensible, to parents and teachers. It is in no way precluded that such new insight may shed impartial light on their own biological inheritance, on the way the family and schools have brought them along, on the time in which they live, and on changes they therefore need now to make in what shall be their own outlook and life-habits.

The all-important goal, when young people have had the thrill of discovering moral or other truths for themselves, having been left free to formulate them with courage and care, is that they shall feel them to be their very own—their own discovery, their own invention, their own choice. And if through utterly uncritical imitation of adult example they have exercised in earlier years their aptitude for action, and through whole-souled trust in adult authority have developed their powers of feeling, they will now place just these powers of feeling and will in the service of their own freely conceived ideal. Such young people will set this ideal before themselves, believe in it, and steadfastly pursue it, with the enthusiasm of full-fledged individuals. In this moment of perfect moral freedom, it will be apparent that the trusting child's earlier imitation, discipleship, and obedience are providing the very substance of present free idealism. It is a single sap that appears first as root and stem, then as leaf, and finally as flower. The flower gives the plant its name, and the flower in this case is individuality, based in the free choice of, love for, active obedience to, what is thought to be right and true. If the earlier rooting and leafage have not been vigorous and uninhibited, the eventual flowering, too, will be stunted.

Young people whose childhoods have been touched by the blight of "critical thinking" will come to the moment of independent insight badly crippled—thought power, lacking foundation, will be easily exhausted. Such young people will be hard put to know what are their own thoughts and what are relics of the years when parents and teachers reasoned with them instead of appealing directly to their instinct for love and obedience. Even if at this later stage they can identify the ideas that they believe to be true—by no means an easy task for one surfeited with rationalizing—they will have difficulty in advancing these ideas to the status of effective ideals. Because skepticism has long since robbed them of part of their hearts, they will now feel unable to embrace enthusiastically even what they have come to understand and believe. For them, the light brought by understanding will shine more like a moon than a sun; it will lack the burning power necessary for creative response. The old habits of incomplete trust and delayed, grudging obedience will prevent them at the crucial moment from bringing themselves promptly and completely into line with what they have decided is best. Though their spirits may be willing, the flesh will be weak. They will present the very picture of unfreedom.

From what has been said, the answer to the second misunderstanding, mentioned earlier, should now be clear. There is no reason why adults, during young people's high school and college years, should not continue to exercise full authority over many aspects of the behavior of those in their care. There is, indeed, every reason why they should do so. How can either home or school demonstrate its concern for good in the world, if not by insisting upon aesthetic and moral standards within the area of its clear responsibility There is room for variety in the ways parents or teachers will state and stick to their standards—they may be pompous or humorous, narrow-minded or broad-minded, harsh or tactful —but how can any who are plainly still charged with educating youth excuse themselves for not standing up in their own households for the qualities of life they prefer?

There is no conflict at all between a high school or college saying to its students, "Your purpose at this stage is to investigate freely and come to your own conclusions," and "While you are engaged in such study, please observe *our* standards of behavior." The students' imperative to examine and conclude cannot be supposed to conflict with their hosts' right to keep order in their own homes according to their own values. Students may disagree and lay plans to run *their* homes, or schools, one day quite differently. They are free to develop such plans in great detail. They should also be free to bring forward, as reasonable suggestions, any changes they would like to propose for the present situation. But nothing in their educations for individuality requires them to be disrespectful or even repetitive in their criticism, to say nothing of insubordination or inciting to disobedience. Their own time of responsibility will be soon at hand. When that time comes, they will appreciate at last why a social climate of order rather than anarchy is desirable. Without social order, *no* one's freedom of moral judgment and initiative will be able to achieve anything that goes beyond itself.

The very premise of responsible authority at any level of education is, of course, freedom of choice: choice for teachers and choice for parents and older students. Only when teachers are free to teach according to their deepest conviction and ultimate values, and when parents and older students are free to enter or stay out of the school where this teaching takes place, can the right relationships develop between authority and freedom, discipline and freedom. If teachers are not free to offer and require what *they* truly think most important, they will never establish the right kind of authority. To the extent that they are themselves unfree to be the creative originators, the true authors, of their educational method, they will fail also to inspire in their students the creative independence that begins with unquestioning respect, love, and obedience. This theme will be developed in the next chapter. A further word, however, needs to be said here about the quality of the authority to be exercised by those who educate children.

As we have indicated, this authority should be decisive. Using a rather cumbersome analogy, we may say that as the power of teachers' example works through the deep desire of early childhood to imitate, adult authority is helping children to *build* their boat; as teachers' inspiration works through children's deep desire to trust and admire, adult authority is helping to fill the boat's sail; and a "hands off" policy on the part of all adult authorities with regard to moralizing and preaching leaves the boats' pilots free, when they are licensed, to step into their crafts, take the tillers, and sail their own courses.

But the concept of authority awakens so many dark suspicions in so many people in our time that we must try to clarify what distinguishes the legitimate function from the illegitimate. It is not social, economic, or academic position, nor is it any personal ability or training, that in the last analysis gives the parent or teacher authority. The children themselves give this authority to adults. With all their hearts, children, pupils, students, *want* to revere and obey their teachers. To a great extent, children give authority to adults whether they deserve it or not. But of course they should deserve it, and under one condition they will. All kinds of people can be good parents and teachers, if only they will accept the obligation of their role. The essential is to grasp with absolute firmness that while children find their authority at first in persons, these persons themselves, being long past childhood, must always look for *their* motives beyond their own personality. The full authority they need and should have derives not from themselves but from the role they are assigned to play. Their authority belongs to the objective function of parenthood and teaching. There can be no indulging of a personal will to power, any more than there can be shirking of the responsible use of power. Parents and teachers should realize that when they shrink from the effort to be worthy of the authority that belongs to their office, and when they shun even the idea of authority, they cut the tap-root of freedom.

Authority calls for discipline—for *discipleship* from those under authority; but only those are worthy to have disciples under personal guidance who are themselves disciples of the impersonal ideal. The more perfectly parents or teachers hold themselves under the discipline of what they feel to be good in itself, the more legitimate power they will have to hold and guide the children entrusted to their care; the more chance they will have to satisfy them in heart and will. The ideal that must guide them in all their educational responsibilities can, of course, be only their own concepts of the necessities of the roles they should be playing. But though parents and teachers may differ concerning the demands of this role, this office, this sacred duty, if they will remain scrupulously obedient to the concept they have chosen for themselves, and which they obey, they will have the measure of authority they need.

Children should and will in any case look up to their parents and teachers; but their obedience will last longer, and they will be gladder in the depths of their souls, if these authorities themselves are looking with the same humble reverence to their own ideals. In the last analysis, adult authorities teach children and youth to obey, only to the extent that they themselves obey. Just this much can they, in fact, actually impart. Their lasting gift to the young, therefore, will be far less the ideas *they* hold dear, and far more the capacity to love the ideas their *children* will eventually choose for themselves—wishing them power to convert these ideas into effective ideals and follow them faithfully through thick and thin.

Love is the golden thread throughout all education for individuality and freedom. Whoever at any stage truly loves, is living the life of freedom, as an individual of integrity. For the youngest child, imitation is active love; for the elementary school pupil, obedience and trust are feeling love; and at adolescence, a burning idealism becomes thinking love. But the all-important love of the young for parents and teachers, which makes later forms of love possible, is a function of these adults' faithfulness to the authority fate asks them to carry. Who shirks the full exercise of this legitimate, indispensable authority fails to educate through love.

10

The Next Step

The criterion of growth is progress towards self-determination; and progress towards self-determination is a prosaic
formula for describing the miracle by which Life enters into
its Kingdom. —*Arnold Toynbee*

WE HAVE BEEN AT PAINS TO SHOW that when individuals
give themselves wholly to the full-fledged *experience* of knowledge—that is, when they devote their energies of feeling and
will to the task of thinking clearly—the realizations to which
they come represent a maximum of self-activity and self-fulfill-
ment, but they also yield the truths of objective reality. We have
noted that what arises under these conditions from the most
private center of individual consciousness is a most public
thing. What emerges is the same for everyone. It is, in fact, the
creative life of reason, which makes the world intelligible because it is the spiritual substance of humanity and world alike.
When human beings are moved by concern for truth to draw
upon their innermost depths, where reason dwells, then in their
thinking, though they have started from diverse standpoints,
they begin at once to converge, to coincide. Precisely through
our most individual efforts of real thinking, we find ourselves
most completely at one with each other, "For the thinking of
the many is in itself a unity."[1] Following these implications of
the private-public mystery of human cognition has helped us to
distinguish good from bad methods of guidance and teaching.

---

1. See Appendix E, Part 2.

Let us use the same light to clarify the relationship between educational institutions as such and the society they serve.

It cannot be too often repeated that education is in many ways the most important single function of modern society. *All* artists, religious leaders, scientists, lawyers, doctors, farmers, teachers, engineers, business people, persons of state—and indeed *all* wives and husbands, *all* mothers and fathers—have spent the long period of their most formative years in school. Because the school years are so decisive for the nation as a whole and because all citizens are taxed to raise the vast sums of money that go to support the schools, society is naturally jealous that education shall be managed in the public interest. This public interest is best served, according to a general opinion throughout the world today, by laws requiring universal support of a state system of schools: that is, schools established by state mandate, financed by taxes, and subject in educational policy and standards to various levels of governmental authority. In America, we speak of the public school as "the cornerstone of democracy."

Literacy is, of course, necessary for an informed electorate; some knowledge and certain skills are needed by all citizens if they are to take their places productively in the economy. We assume that public schools are necessary to achieve these goals. Yet obviously such ends do not require state-supported and state-controlled systems of education, since independent schools of many varieties have shown themselves easily capable of supplying these minimal requirements and much besides. The more basic reason, it seems, why during several centuries the West has focused its hope upon state school systems, why these have been held to be a social necessity, and why—no matter how badly these schools may disappoint practical as well as spiritual needs—they are still protected with dogmatic, almost religious fervor, lies in a specific fear. This fear has been growing throughout the modern era. It has paralleled the increase of intellectualistic, egoistic materialism and the decline of positive moral-aesthetic-religious experience in Western culture. What we rightly fear are the socially destructive consequences of this egoism.

Egoism on the one hand, and on the other hand the fear of egoism, arise when we pay more attention to the private person in whom thought takes place than to the content of that thought, which is public reality. We shall not find the cause of egoism in the one mind that lives in everyone, but in the many bodies that seek to appropriate this mind. As we have indicated throughout this book, an age that believes "private" physical brains are meant to produce and possess rather than be tamed by thinking will be an age that has everything to fear from egoism. It will instinctively try to build an "OK Corral" to contain the antisocial impulses that are sure to issue from all those self-seeking brains. Believing there is nothing that draws thinking people of their *own* accord toward harmony, the materialistic society will never cease trying to guarantee social cohesion by the imposition of laws: primarily by laws touching the control of education.

Egoism in its wholesome form as individual judgment and enterprise is rightly admired and fostered in America today; but in the form of selfishness and anarchy it is rightly feared. The anarchical form of self-will appears in civil life as corruption and disorder; in economic life as the competitive exploitation of nature and of each other. We *could* try to understand exactly where, and how, justified individualism turns into unjustified egoism, so that we might pinpoint the root-cause of this greatest of all sicknesses of the modern age, and direct our cure to that. Instead, we live superstitiously under a generalized fear that fails to distinguish between sick and healthy forms of individualism, and we cling to an educational remedy that threatens to make the sick form incurable.

Harmonious unity is either basic to human nature, needing only to be awakened in the depths of individual souls, or else we are ultimately competing organisms that must always be conditioned and controlled from without. It is this latter, mostly unconscious supposition that leads to the public school system, with its increasingly centralized direction by state and federal authorities. The former supposition calls rather for progressive decentralization of the public schools, until each and every school in the land achieves autonomy in its policy and practices: that is, until it becomes a fully independent, self-directing institution.

A misunderstanding of the will to freedom has again and again in this permissive century persuaded millions of parents and teachers that children at the earliest ages should be encouraged to evaluate and choose what they want and what they will do. But it is not school children who need or can use this kind of freedom; for as we have shown earlier, it actually leads them away from freedom. Not immature students in their *learning*, but mature teachers in their *teaching* are those who should be free. Upon the protection of teachers' freedom, the future of our society will depend. For society, it is education as a whole, and for education it is the teacher in particular, that must be recognized as the goose who lays the golden eggs. All teachers, from nursery through college, must be permitted to build their educational initiatives, their methods, upon freely arrived-at insights, following their own best judgments.

Such freedom for teachers requires, of course, a matching freedom for parents. Parents should also be free to act upon their own judgment concerning the values they want for their children. While it is undeniable that teachers teach best when they are free to determine what and how they will teach—that is, free to offer society their unique service in the same way that

artists, inventors, engineers, architects, ministers, or doctors offer their creations and counsel—parents should be equally free
to take or to leave the teaching offered.

The regeneration of modern society awaits the freeing of authority for teachers and choice for parents. It is hardly exagger-
ation to say that most of the ills of Western culture today, most
of the unsolved problems, can be traced back to the fatal tie between education and government. The unworkability of this tie
cannot be overstated. As inevitably as perverse forms of egoism
will continue to increase so long as most schools are state
schools, just so inevitably will society move to bring these
schools ever more completely under political dominion, in the
vain effort to curb such egoism. This closing spiral leads inevitably to the totalitarian state, whose first act, witnessed frequently in this century, is to take absolute charge of all
educational agencies.

It is a mistake to believe that state-controlled curriculums, evaluation procedures, and methods of training and certifying teachers, are bad in a dictatorship but good in a democracy. Our
American public schools, though some efficiency, discipline, intellectual standards, and moral content still appear in them here
and there, are disappointing the great hopes we have placed in
them. They show no signs, however, of being able to halt their
growing apathy and demoralization They show every sign of fall-
ing into conditions that will seem to justify ever greater control
by the states. Looking at the matter from the viewpoint of the
motivation of teachers, we can see that hopes for the state school
system in America as a disciplined, dynamic, creative agency have
no chance of being realized. Looking at modern history in other
lands, we can see that the state school system has been both an
easy captive and a ready conductor of totalitarian mind control.
Our task in the present context cannot be to examine all the
problems that a new way of handling the control and support

of education will raise. None of these problems is unsolvable; the unsolvable problems are the ones arising from the existing arrangements, from the fundamentally unsound and unworkable idea that education can ever be considered a legitimate function of the state. In the long run, a right thought will always be easier to implement than a wrong one, and we may trust that in practical life events will always conspire to aid the concept that takes account of primary truth. The primary truth that concerns us here is that the time has come for American education to grow-up. From now on, education must steadily, progressively, and as rapidly as possible come free from external controls. It must be permitted to develop its own policies and its own strength. Only under these conditions will it have any chance of bringing to our society the new life it so badly needs.

When we speak of education being free to follow its own prompting, we have in mind, of course, individual teachers and faculties of teachers, not administrators, trustees, or other officials, if these are not also functioning actively as teachers. When teachers work from their own insight and conscience, from their devotion to the particular children in their classes, from enthusiasm for the particular subjects they are teaching, and from the wish to serve the time in which they live, they will draw forth all these same qualities from children. When the educational enterprise as a whole is of their own making, so that they know themselves to be unmistakably responsible for it, no one will be more concerned than precisely teachers themselves to find the solution to their problems, down to the last practical detail. Only when teachers and principal teachers are free to manage the administrative and broader public aspects of their own educational institutions, in the same spirit as they manage teaching itself, will they gain a firm footing in the practical realities of contemporary society. Self-governing schools will be community builders, and in the communities with which they will tend to surround themselves, social feeling and confidence in the power of education to contribute to society will take on for teachers, parents, and students a vital intensity presently unimagined.

One cannot overestimate the moral weakness, the social apathy, the dull life-estrangement and even resentment that enter the children of today, the citizens of tomorrow, from teachers who are essentially unresponsible for the content and method of their teaching.

"Public" education is by its nature politicized. Yet in a democracy politics should concern itself not with intellectual and spiritual questions but only with the equitable adjustment of rights and duties, the establishment of fair relationships among citizens, and the protection of their life in common. People should be casting their equal votes only on matters where they *are* equal: that is, on purely human questions where their preferences and judgment deserve equal consideration. But in the field of education one is dealing also and primarily with specific talents, judgments, and initiatives. The general laws that arise from political consensus have nothing to say about such individual matters. It seems obvious that since education finds its very substance in the investigation of truth, in the cultivation of aesthetic, moral, and religious values, legal-political action is not fitted to intervene. To introduce political procedures and power into the quest for ultimate values, as we are foolishly proud of doing at the present time under the name of democratic process, community control, and the like, is to cripple education: indeed, to take the heart out of the striving of both teachers and students.

What gives both teachers and students heart is precisely their sense of ultimate values. The reason modern youth is by turns so apathetic and so violent, so bewildered and so bitter, is that it has done all its growing up in public schools whose teachers were compelled to ignore the deepest values. We do not wish at this point to accent any particular value but rather the general idea of *that which is ultimate.* The foundation upon which a sound structure of any kind is built may be called an ultimate. And the goal toward which anyone's striving is directed—as all plants grow toward the sun—is an ultimate. How, then, can schools develop standards worthy of the name, when they must transmit subject matter and skills without giving their students a clear orientation with respect to foundations and goals—without building upon freely chosen allegiance to the values, including certainly and by all means the religious values, that make human life ultimately worth living? Apart from ultimate values, how can schools establish effective priorities for themselves or their students? Such a confused educational process, neutral-to-negative toward highest and deepest truths, will either convince the young that life has no meaning, in which case the will-to-live begins to die, or it will cause the young to look for meaning in places where it cannot be found, for example in the selfish pursuit of personal pleasures and economic or political power.

A discussion of "ultimate values" remains for most people too abstract to be really thought about, unless the discussion centers on religion. Then the issue usually becomes so charged with emotion that it still cannot be thought about effectively. Let us, however, not dodge the issue of religious values. All education that is capable of enlisting teachers' best energies and of giving their pupils the bread of life they long for and without which other bread does not nourish, must be regarded as religious.[2] It need not be dogmatic or ritualistic, or in any way affiliated with a church or

---

2. See Appendix G, Part 1.

sect; but it cannot avoid questions of higher forms of cognition, of the reality of the human soul and spirit, of life beyond the bodily, of spiritual beings above and below humanity, of a spiritual concept of the evolution of the kingdoms of nature, of destiny, and of God. Sunday school teachers cannot cope with such problems effectively, in their hour a week, apart from the lore of history and the sciences of nature. Neither are parents who have been educated in the religiously neutralized public school in a good position to answer their children's questions on these matters. Such questions arise for children every day, out of the study of art, of nature, of history, of world events. They arise, too, over the years, out of human experiences and interactions in the classroom. And when they arise among the children, teachers know full well that the next move is theirs. It will be their duty either to respond to such inquiries out of their careful but open judgment—or to evade them because spiritual questions are in the school considered illegitimate, in bad taste, and even illegal.

All significant education must be free to give honest answers to questions about ultimate values. Since atmosphere and example carry still more weight than words, this freedom must extend to the whole style and mood of school life. Education must be free to develop both out of and toward religious experience. It cannot be severed from religion, if we understand religion as deepest experience of the human soul rather than as something dogmatic or institutional. Because all education is in this sense religious (even when it chooses to be agnostic or even antireligious), we must come to recognize that the wall of separation that has rightly been raised between all forms of religion and the state should be raised also between all forms of education and the state.

The true and necessary meaning of the First Amendment to the Constitution of the United States of America would be clearer were it further amended to read, "There shall be no law respecting an establishment of cultural-spiritual conviction or initiative (as in science, art, religion, *and education*) or preventing the free exercise thereof."[3]

We must observe once again that when a society forecloses the freedom to share in the classrooms the more delicate experiences of the soul, the greater mysteries of the inquiring mind, the ultimates of human existence, really heartfelt and fully conscientious thinking of every kind is undone at the same time. The humanity goes out of it, it becomes superficial and technical. These are the very traits that spell materialism, the materialism that spawns the egoism we so rightly fear. When we do not put heart and soul into thinking, so that we know for sure what real thinking is, and know with equal certainty that such thought is not a private matter but belongs to the very nature of things, we can easily be persuaded that the content of thinking is determined in any way others may wish to suggest—by genetic, molecular, electrical, or "unknown" influences. We can be persuaded that it is not our own integrity, but our unique brain that is doing the thinking, that thought *must* therefore be biased, and that by this fact we are cut off from any really basic sharing of one world and one mind with each other.

Only what is intrinsically, ultimately worthwhile draws out the full effort of crystal-clear consciousness that is thinking-according-to-truth. This kind of thinking perceives and feels that truth is really one. When people earnestly, modestly, seek their judgment from this One, this single *holy spirit* of truth, they experience what actually knits humanity together. Whatever fails, therefore, to activate human consciousness to its full depth, limiting it to superficial knowledge and skills, has the effect in the first place of taking the heart out of human beings, and in the

---

3. See Appendix G., Part 2.

second place, of setting people against each other. The "whatever" that is having just these drastic consequences today is a school system that has full charge of children during the time when they should be learning to think, yet that cannot speak of the things that are most important to be thought about and felt.

We have earlier spoken repeatedly about what education can do to foster the love of nature. Such love may be kindled by the beauty of natural forms, or the moral values they exemplify; it may arise from the very mathematics of natural processes; but whatever the starting-point, there will be no *lasting* wonder, no *deeper* caring, unless immediate things suggest ultimates.

Our love of the nature that surrounds us depends in the last analysis upon our ability to find a certain real kinship with all its manifestations. This ability derives from a spiritual outlook upon life. But in modern times such an outlook cannot be legislated, or bought, or in any way demanded. It can be approached only in the way here suggested: by giving freedom to the schools. Though we cannot ask of teachers, however desirable that might seem, to believe that spiritual reality underlies the whole of creation, we *can* make arrangements that will elicit from teachers as they introduce world reality to their students, their own spiritual best; so that they will teach at least from heartfelt conviction, and fully human enthusiasm.

To trace a cause-effect relationship between the progressive de-spiritualization of our time and such major problems as the plundering and pollution of an unloved environment is not hard. Only if we ascribe to American education an inconsequential role can we say that it has but "reflected" this de-spiritualization. If we regard the schools as an important formative influence, we must admit in the first place that they have done very much to bring about the loss of spirit, and in the second place that we must look to them for the necessary changes if a new spirit is to enter American culture. Yet at the same time we must also remain within the realm of the possible. It would be idle to exhort or try to compel American teachers to "restore spirituality" to their curriculum and methods. They would rightly rebel in the name of freedom. And in any case the task of restoring spirituality is not something that can be done at second hand, from outside or above, by committee or by edict. It must be achieved at first hand by the free choice and effort of each teacher and student.

There is no educational arrangement that will guarantee the renewal of a spiritual world-concept; but there is one that will move in that direction. We can make sure that education will become, if not immediately spiritual, at least spirited. We may expect a wholly new spiritedness in the educational community when we permit freedom of initiative to develop among teachers and at the same time support freedom of choice among parents. Full freedom to transform what presently exists is the only way to attract enterprising men and women to teaching. Their spirited efforts, beginning no doubt with simple changes but going on surely to major departures and transformations, will send life surging again through students, and from students into the nation.

One could, of course, at this point raise a question. If liberation can give us spirited teachers, how does one account for the less than spirited performance at present of some teachers in independent schools?

The so-called independent school is rarely independent in the sense we have in mind, because teachers in it are too seldom really free to probe and heed their own conscience. Because such schools require tuition fees, citizens who are already paying taxes for the public school often cannot afford them; so it is a wealthier clientele which supports and controls policy in many non-public schools. Too often this clientele has no clearer ideas about how freedom is related to a spirited education than do most public school parents. Too often it assumes that good teachers can be hired, that pressure and pay will get the most out of them, and that the purpose of the whole enterprise has little to do with freedom. Most independent schools knuckle under to the same pressures that spell unfreedom for public schools: that is, the requirements of schools farther up the line. These requirements, be it said, often do not represent the deeply considered best judgment of those actually teaching on the higher levels, but rather they can be traced back to dictates that come from still higher up, or from outside education—in the last analysis usually from special business and professional interests or from governmental efforts to standardize quality. As all such requirements tend to stereotypes, so do the methods of preparing to meet them.

In most non-public schools, even as in public schools, the idea that the teacher should be the real author and responsible agent in education has scarcely dawned. For both, despite their claims to professionalism, teachers are hired help who serve the purposes set for them—whether by the state, the church, business interests, or parents of position and power. Private school and college faculties no more question the appropriateness of trustees setting ultimate policy than parochial teachers question the church hierarchy above them, or public schools the board of education. In every case, there is theoretical acceptance, even while there is also practical unhappiness, that those who are themselves not teaching should ultimately control the content, aims, and methods of the education offered.

The occasional rebellions of teaching staffs are seldom impressive, because these demonstrations are made not out of a wish to carry the full responsibility for education, but rather to settle certain grievances, or for the sake of shorter hours, fewer duties, and more pay. Teachers hardly imagine that the reason they feel so strongly about such goals is that their really primary interest has been ignored: namely, their desire to be decisively, creatively free. The great unions that increasingly speak for teachers take for granted limitations that should not be taken for granted. They are demanding about external prerogatives, yet it seems not to occur to them that teachers should really be in charge of their own affairs. The monolithic power of unions depends apparently upon maintenance of the monolithic state school system. Both this system and the unions place the individual teacher and the individual school faculty almost last on the list of policy-shapers.

Of course, it is true that in a materialistic epoch even the freedom to control their own school will not necessarily elicit from teachers a very spirited response. Materialism, here as elsewhere, is the greatest imaginable dampener of spirits. There is no doubt that for real caring, real fire, and real conscientiousness to live in teachers, they need more than bare "freedom." They need insight and guidance also, which come from a spiritual concept of life. Although such concepts exist, the tragedy is that they have no chance—in schools that remain dominated by church dogma, economic power, or the voting power of a divided community—to take effect promptly, as soon as they have shown their worth to the teaching staff. What chance is there of a spiritualizing leaven working strongly enough and swiftly enough to save our civilization, unless each school faculty, after comparing notes with others, is autonomous enough to change as soon and as thoroughly as it finds good reasons to change?

Education is just being born. Its need for autonomy arises urgently from its own nature. This urgency comes to expression, however, in devious ways, often in mistaken attempts to give students premature control over their own schooling, or in blind allegiance to the idea of iron-clad tenure for teachers, or in conflict between teaching faculties and administrative staffs. But the case is seldom stated plainly or set in context, for teachers themselves don't know their own mind in the matter. Independent schools, for all their claims to freedom, generally do not face the issue. Parochial schools are more impassioned in claiming their right to public support than in defending the necessity of education to be free. They seem willing to strike bargains that will seriously diminish even their present degree of freedom.

Some on the far right of economic theory are glad to espouse libertarianism in any form, but they confuse schools with businesses conducted for profit. They have a sound feeling for enterprise, one that does indeed apply to the issue of initiative and choice in education; but they cancel this plus with a minus. They seemingly have no notion of why the offerings of religion, art, science, and education could and should go beyond the laws of property and bartering. The market objectives of business that presently so emphasize price and profit, and that depend so heavily upon an advertising that tends to deceive even while it informs, would infuse into education motives and methods that would ultimately do more harm than good. Education should always concern itself with what can be given rather than what can be gotten, and with what is good and true rather than what will sell.

That education is not primarily a commercial enterprise is obvious from the fact that in business dealings every product is sold for a price. In education, however, as in religion, the basic transaction is much more one of reciprocal giving. The school makes its offering, and in return—because of tuition grants, annual giving, endowment, and the like, none of which plays any part in ordinary market transactions—one family will offer $40, another $400, and a third $4,000. The tuition fees charged by independent schools, colleges, and universities are therefore really misleading. They carry business habits of thought into a realm where they do not apply. The impression they give that an educational "product" is being "bought" at its "price" is essentially false.

In educational circles, there is a very widespread realization that capable, deserving students should no more be kept out of school simply because they cannot pay tuition than religious seekers would be barred from church because they do not have the price of a ticket. In private schools, philanthropy enables many to attend on the basis of "scholarships." In public schools, the tax levy enables all children to attend, as we misleadingly say, "free." Any given stage in schooling has, in effect, many prices and no price. We must conclude that the arcane concept of price is out of place in what concerns the essence of the educational process.

One comes to the same conclusion by another route when one notes that in things economic, to give away goods or property is to have less. To impart or give away spiritual goods, on the other hand, is to have more. In things cultural and spiritual, division multiplies like the Gospel loaves and fishes. Not getting but giving must be the motive here.[4] One must believe that increasing recognition of education's need for autonomy will bring with it the realization that our economic bookkeeping needs another category. Among the groupings that account for where money is and what it is doing there should be a major new column: "Free Gifts." Much money is involved in buying and selling, in savings, in loans, and in investments—and the new category should be of similar size. It should represent the whole substance of the support freely given to cultural-spiritual activities. If a society may be likened to a plant, we can visualize some aspects of the economy as resembling roots that establish

---

4. See Appendix G, Part 2.

the society materially in nature. Other aspects, the leaf-and-stem function, may be seen as purely human interchanges, "services" rendered to people by other people. Education, religion, science, and art go beyond such human services. In spiritual matters, we live by grace under a higher law. Teachers and preachers, artists and scientists, reach beyond the known or possessed, to become conductors for the possible lightning of inspiration. Through them new streams of will and wisdom and love enter into the ordinary life of humanity. But these new strengths are not to be commanded, nor can they be purchased. They are *given* to human beings from above as gifts of blessing. The proper response is counter-gifts of gratitude. Thus, this aspect of the plant that is society seems to rise above the leafy transactions of purely human service into the blossom, fruit, and seed of a higher give-and-take. When money enters this stage, it is somehow transformed. The bartering, the *quid pro quo* transaction, falls away.

If we may speak a little wildly, let us try to characterize the relationship between the economy of a society and the entirety of its spiritual-cultural life in some such way as the following. The economy represents all efforts that provide people with livelihoods and living conditions. But once their living is secure, what will people live *for?* They have strength remaining, and the wish to make further efforts. Will these go only to assure a constantly rising standard of living; or will they not be far better directed to fulfill the ultimate purpose, the flowering, of existence? Such *final* purposes are comprised by the spiritual-cultural aspect of life in all its variety.[5] If we view matters in this way, we can imagine that while the economic substance of a society is to

---

5. "The true thrift is always to spend on the higher plane; to invest and invest, with keener avarice, that [we] may spend in spiritual creation and not in augmenting animal existence."—Emerson, *Wealth*, p. 711.

be achieved by digging into material existence as a plant strikes its roots into Earth, there comes a time when a major portion of the substance drawn from Earth should be lifted up, sacrificed as it were: to undergo transformation even as green plant leaves are changed by the sun into flowers and fruit. And as the plant, out of this transformation, gains the seeds of its renewal, so a society gains the new wisdom and power that will make its future. Once again we are reminded of Goethe's "Die and become!" The plant of this year gives its whole strength into the seed for next year. The material economy of people should also give of its substance, to receive gifts in return that will make further life worthwhile: gifts of the spirit that come to meet it out of science, art, religion, and education.

It was Christ's saying that "Except a grain of wheat fall into the ground and die, it abideth alone: but if it die, it bringeth forth much fruit." We read the same meaning into the idea that unless economic values are offered freely in support of cultural-spiritual activities and institutions, and in this sense "die," they will not find any adequate way to achieve the fruit that is human fulfillment and the renewal of society. It appears to us that the whole distillate from humanity's economic earnings should at some point be yielded up, somehow undergo a kind of discontinuity, at that stage where the market exchange of commodities and services ends and the spiritual give-and-take begins. Out of this momentary death of economic values, humankind would receive its new lease on life, its ability to create new values.

How this naive way of looking at the matter could be stated in proper language—by an economist who chose to find a useful lead in it—I have no idea. If all money *eventually* became gift money, and gift money were the end of the road as it were, then economists would have to invent a way in which gift money could become old money, or old money gift money;

and then as this money entered the gift process, it would die: to be reborn as new money with which a new circle of economic activity could begin. Such a fantasy, at least its statement in this form, may be foolishness, yet it will have served its purpose if it has prolonged attention to our serious proposal that education *not* be paid for as are purely economic commodities. Though some may be confused or annoyed by the images used in this effort to break out of usual thought habits in discussing the support of education—when education shall have been granted the freedom it requires—and in trying to suggest the fallacy of certain libertarian ideas about education as a free-enterprise business, these images are meant, of course, to be no more than suggestive. One need not take offense at the crudeness of a sign, if it serves to point the right direction.

Leaving aside the unsolved, scarcely as yet imagined, problem of how autonomous spiritual-cultural activity, education above all, should ultimately receive support from a nation's economy, some features of the relationship are clear. Whatever the arrangements in education may be, they should facilitate as far as possible the free initiative of teachers and parents. They should take account of and give expression to the motives of a) creative-offering-according-to-ability and b) grateful-response-according-to-means. Bureaucratic intermediary steps, where both money and freedom are lost, should be held to a minimum. Also to be avoided is the impression that "they," the powers that be, are taking care of us, rather than that we as individual human beings, through the free combinations into which we enter, ourselves supply the power and the guidance for education. We should build upon the definite assumption that the way to raise more money is not to increase demands but to permit more freedom for initiative and choice. The enthusiasm generated by true cultural freedom will show itself able to draw forth money that taxes will never extract; and if taxes there must be, for a time, these will be paid the more willingly, the more schools can be freely chosen. If there is money enough for all children in the present state system, there will be substantially more available, I should guess, when schools become independent. An appropriate distribution of this money is surely not beyond the power of good judgment and modern techniques.

Let us be absolutely clear above all that there is no use trying to give freedom with one hand while taking it away with the other. If it seems desirable as a beginning to pay for independence in education by vouchers, let us not hedge them with laws and limits that will destroy the freedom presently enjoyed by the schools who will be induced to accept these vouchers. Every plan that has a chance of succeeding must be based on recognition that if the sense of moral responsibility does not arise freely, it can never be imposed by legislative mandates.

There was a time when we felt an urgent need for an instrument that would serve to melt down cultural differences and amalgamate an extraordinarily diverse immigrant population within a common understanding and a national spirit. Whether or not we were under an illusion then concerning our actual need, and concerning the propriety of using the public schools as this instrument, times have changed. The need today is not for a "melting pot," but for an agency of differentiation and individuation. The public school has not produced national harmony, pride, or esprit de corps. Though many would blame quite other factors for the loss of morale and hope, of wisdom and energy, and of human community in our nation, the public schools cannot accept praise at one moment, as the very cornerstone of our democracy, without staying to take their central share of blame for the predicament in which our democracy now finds itself. America is proud of its rugged individualism; but on all sides we see the prevalence of conformity, confusion, and fear. The culture of America lacks differentiation and color; it is becoming characterless in essence as in appearance. We are being homogenized by the techniques of mass production, techniques that demand uniformity of materials and specifications, permitting the smooth interchangeability of parts. The mass media—magazines and newspapers, radio and TV, movies—do their part in erasing individuality. Big business, big labor, big government, and big bombs all belittle the desires and decisions of single persons. Each takes some of the starch out of really rugged individualism, replacing it with a weak egoism that when incited is querulous and cantankerous enough, but not to be depended upon for either initiative or staying power. This principle of dealing with masses instead of with individuals has unduly shaped our schools, and the men and women who emerge from them. At the present time, big education is a *focus* for the baleful effect of all the other forms of bigness that tend to leave Americans bewildered and helpless.

We present-day Americans need individuation. We need the example of moral courage. Children should be going to schools whose teachers are self-starting prime movers. Contrary to popular opinion, the diversity of such schools will not weaken but will greatly strengthen social cohesion. The education of Americans will not need to homogenize the unique contributions of language and customs that many who become citizens bring with them from other parts of the world. It will recognize that the very strongest force for national unity is to be achieved not by institutions of mass conditioning and mind control but by the gratitude free individuals feel toward the society that gives them leave to pursue distinctive cultural values in their own way.

A most heartening forward step in American education at

the moment is one that starts from where we are, from the public schools, and shows how the principle of autonomy can at least begin to be activated in them. Very recently, many communities across the nation have come to realize that their several elementary or secondary schools need not be all alike. The board of education need not hold them to one policy; there can be alternatives. Those who want to get the full benefit of putting the teacher in charge, and those who believe the children know best what will make them prosper, need not fight to see who will capture control of across-the-board policy.[6] They can feel friendly toward each other, develop a cordial human solidarity with each other, over the fact that pluralistic educational arrangements permit them to follow different life-strategies within their same community. Were this recognition of the equal rights of alternative schools encouraged to develop self-consistently to its only reasonable conclusion, it would soon include non-public schools. It would indeed assimilate public to non-public schools rather than the other way around; and so we should have made a practical start for the long overdue evolution toward complete cultural-spiritual freedom in education.

---

6. "As governmental pressure toward unity becomes greater, so strife becomes more bitter as to whose unity it shall be." —Justice Robert H. Jackson cited in Commager, *Living Ideas in America*, p. 544.

Afterword

Outlook for America

"What is freedom?" the American asked.
"Freedom?" said the Russian. He hesitated for a moment,
but without taking his eyes off the American. "Freedom,"
he said, "is knowing how to help the other fellow. It is
brotherhood." —*Russell W. Davenport*

EDUCATION IS BASIC to the vitality of a nation. Basic to education is the experience of knowledge. Basic to the living, full-fledged experience of knowledge is understanding of the subjective-objective nature of thought. An understanding of the nature of thought leads to confidence that if it is left free to deepen its own resources, employing heart and will, thinking becomes spirited. And it begins to grow by its very nature toward a spiritual conception of reality. Such a conception prepares an individual to be fully active in a meaningful world felt to be home: a world that awakens love and quickens fellowship in its inhabitants.

If America, through setting education free from *external* restraints and compulsions, can achieve the renewal of spiritual insight and activity, it will have both the right and the strength to complete that stage of historical evolution that, by progressive steps for some thousands of years, has moved the leadership of nations ever farther toward the West. It can regain its morale, develop a simpler, happier life that is not too expensive for the

Earth to support, and achieve brotherhood in humanity on the basis of a lofty, disciplined concept of individual freedom. Despite all its mistakes, blemishes, and shortcomings, America still leads the nations of today's world. They all want what is good in her. When America falters or does wrong, the sad effects are worldwide.

But America is faltering. Those who look to us observe that we ourselves do not know where to look. Yet while we in America ponder and delay dealing with the problem of decadence in our culture, some parts of the Eastern world have become extraordinarily active. The gaze of our youth wanders ignorantly from what is best in the Western heritage. In its disappointment, it shows understandable signs of turning toward the East—to India, Japan, and China—for both spiritual teachings and practical example.

There can hardly be a greater contrast than that between the almost religious communalism of the East and the allegedly rugged individualism of modern America: the rigor of self-sacrifice there (whether for the most part willing or not), affluent self-indulgence here. Most Americans still suppose that the advantage lies all with us, but does it? As the Western world feels the helplessness of its own predominantly material, technological, economic orientation to master soul sickness and social distemper as these are appearing in depressions, addictions, criminality, the dissolving of moral values, and the whole tide of destructive behavior afflicting millions of the younger generation—what is to prevent us from being drawn quite out of our own orbit?

The answer to this question lies in the *spiritual* heritage of the West, the indispensable value of its special striving in the evolution of all humankind. But this answer will have force only so long as Western culture honors what is best in the heritage handed down to it from both Europe and the East in times past, understands this heritage, and summons the will in modern times to complete what was thus begun. Destiny will surely protect what is progressive, but how can it fail to withdraw its favor from a people grown spiritually obtuse, dissolute, and selfish? If the Earth planet is to provide a place for the future of human evolution, destiny cannot permit the continued dominance of a civilization such as ours is becoming, which rapaciously devours irreplaceable Earth resources for spiritually meaningless purposes.

The essential difference between on the one hand America, and on the other hand the awakening Eastern peoples, lies in their different attitudes toward the human ego. While America emphasizes individual differences and self-seeking enterprise, Eastern nations tend to glorify the submergence of personal goals in the commonweal. America believes it will be well governed when everyone can follow their own persuasion in pursuit of their own fulfillment. In the Eastern world, the concept that human welfare depends upon what all do together is both instinctive and consciously supported. The feeling is for one organism, one great family. It is in this sense that communism has taken deepest root and held on longest in that part of the world.

One cannot say that either ideal is wholly wrong. Under both —what is perverse in the American development and regressive in the Chinese, for example—one can discern positive values waiting to be realized. If an America will set the example, showing how fully modern individuals who have left the old *group soul* behind *can* nevertheless achieve real solidarity with one another, no doubt a China *can* be inspired to begin to evolve, from its presently engineered and enforced communalism, to a real trust in freedom for individuality.

Disastrous wrong could enter only if China were not to seek such individual freedom, and if America were not to achieve this community among free people who out of their own un-forced initiative choose to live in harmony with each other and with the Earth. When the West has come of age, there can be no doubt that it will, and should, join hands with the reawak-ened East, to make one world. But this fruition cannot be has-tened, lest what should be the glad union of equals who complement each other suddenly becomes the bloodiest strug-gle in history—to see which shall dominate. In such a struggle, neither East nor West could rightly win, for neither would yet have fulfilled the progressive requirements of its own destiny.

The meaning of the progressive impulse in history that has led steadily away from the East toward the West, leaving the former relatively quiescent while activating the latter has become clear-er with each successive civilization:

Assyria/Babylonia/Chaldea-Egypt, Greece-Rome, Central/Western Europe, and now America. Advancing gradually from the unsurveyably vast landmass of Asia into the concentrated, sharply characterized peninsula of Europe, with its still smaller sub-peninsulas of Greece, Italy, Spain, France, Scandinavia, and reaching a kind of endpoint, a seeming *ne plus ultra* of def-inition in the British Isles, the culture of humankind has taken successive steps away from generalized group experience and toward individuation. The Anglo-Saxon, libertarian ego-im-pulse was carried at last across the Atlantic to America. The Western course of humanity's progress toward individual au-tonomy, or self-determination, has now reached its most criti-cal stage. What we in America do at this point will serve to fulfill or abort, for who knows how long, the entire historical evolution.

It seems plain that on one condition only can America over-come the shame of recent defeats, regain justifiable confidence, and find moral strength to repel both the magnetism and the threat of Eastern communist-communalist impulses. *We must gain insight into the problem, the riddle, of human individuality.* This separate individuality must find depth there where it opens again freely into the universal. At that level, materialism will allow itself to be lifted by the spiritual.

The historical descent into materialism has served one great purpose. It has made possible the emergence of distinct personalities out of the all-creative Ground of Being. As the one primordial Spirit, in the beginnings of human evolution, came to be ever more deeply absorbed into human bodies, separate centers of consciousness and self-determination could arise. But the cost of this forward step has been that darkening of the Spirit by its ever deeper descent into the material body that we call the Fall of Man; and the danger is that humanity will not take the path of redemption—whose time must come and has come, if the Fall is not to be final. For the self-will of a self-conscious individual can be deluded into thinking that the body actually does come first, as the seeming source out of which mind and soul with their allegedly lesser realities have sprung, and that bodies therefore naturally and rightly set the goals for which the so-called inner self in its self-interest should scheme.

Were humanity not to overcome this temporary scientific illusion, the Creative Principle would be torn apart and devoured by its own progeny. A war of God's creation against itself must ensue, setting Man against Man, Man against nature, Man against God.

But if the individuality, who arises when a particular body becomes the habitation of universal Spirit, were to recognize that its origin, the creative factor in it, derives from above, not from below, then events would take an altogether different course. Then, instead of the dismemberment of the divinely creative, there would be the miracle of its renewal and increase here on Earth. The harmonious interaction of independently active men and women would carry on the work of creation in the beauty of its first and still essential meaning. The work would proceed freely from many independent centers but always to the greater glory of the whole.

We have examined the private-public mystery of human individuality as it concerns several aspects of education. But because America is above all proud of her economic system, its right application should be sought also and especially there. America must replace a false economic mystery with a true. It is surely false that "the market place" miraculously transforms self-seeking into common welfare, and that when each works primarily for the personal pay or profit involved—abundance for *all* will be zestfully created and happily distributed. Not even the market place can conjure peace and plenty out of egoism's will to extract and appropriate.

The true mystery of free enterprise lies in what we have seen to be the nature of freedom itself. One is free when the public nature awakens generously within one's private being: when one acts from an upbuilding, generous love for the action one will perform. Such love arises only when the action seems to the individual intrinsically right and good. Though intrinsic value be privately ascertained, it always has a public reference. One loves a deed, economic as well as any other, when it is done not only in one's own style but in the best style, and it expresses not only a personal impulse but one that clearly contributes to the benefit of others. To "enterprise" freely is to act not as one bound by, but as one liberated from, selfishness—aiming always to contribute one's own good to the general good. One asks: What is the good thing, the right and beneficial thing, that I want to do and can do? Though one ask this question in private, of oneself alone, it is one's universal part that answers. What this part decides upon will surely contribute to peace and plenty.

When enterprising men and women make their contribution to world economy in this manner, the market *can* work its miracle.

America has grown great economically, I believe, mainly because her citizens have so often acted otherwise than *laissez faire* capitalism theorizes. They have *enjoyed* working. They have frequently been more interested in the excellence than in the earnings of their deeds. Again and again, they have been sympathetic, kind-hearted, and generous toward their own people and toward others in the world who were in distress. They have been comparatively open-minded, and ready to improve their ways of doing things. All these are universal factors. It is the universality of such motives and qualities that has conjured general prosperity out of "private" enterprise. But it is the ever more prevalent substitution of a really private, selfishly blind concept of individuality that is beginning to cause the American enterprise system, at times now, to seem so helpless—somehow outdated—increasingly both harmful and helpless.

Because we are really entering into freedom, the inherited virtues of an older day must be built up again from the very ground in our own day, and by each individual. This renewal should begin in education. The present book has been an attempt to remind us of where we stand and where we are going in the matter of sound and unsound forms of individualism. The course of history leads one to suppose that finding the clue to true human brotherhood, precisely through deepening the concept and experience of individual freedom, has been reserved for "Western culture," but the time that remains within which our present way of life can still be allowed to wander under the spell of egoism is obviously almost spent.

While an interval of grace remains, we must hope America will decide that what ought to happen for the benefit of all humankind, can happen. Our hope and trust, however, should arise from a vision of our own: the vision of the example and achievement set two thousand years ago by the great Inaugurator, the Redeemer, who showed humanity the future of genuine individualism. As the Prototype of development for human beings of all races, colors, and creeds, He still works—doubtless, now more than ever—to *redeem individuality*. He brings humankind's historical descent into matter to its right recovery and world-transforming fruition.

APPENDICES

APPENDIX A

Rudolf Steiner

The central statement of Rudolf Steiner's epistemology appears in his *Theory of Knowledge,* and especially *Intuitive Thinking as a Spiritual Path.*

> Trained in the natural sciences in Vienna, Steiner edited Goethe's scientific writings, in the Berlin Stuttgart edition (1882-1897). He also participated in the editing of the Weimar edition, which still stands as definitive. He then proceeded to apply and develop the Goethian philosophy of science in numerous fields of learning—physics, chemistry medicine, zoology, botany, history, philology, religion, Christology, scriptural interpretation, and so forth. He demonstrated by his enormous works that the Goethian scientific thesis is true: that whenever we can win our way, in a scientific spirit, to processes of living thought, it is possible then to enter into and understand mysteries that the natural sciences, as hitherto practiced, cannot reach. Steiner's life and works constitute a refutation of modern agnosticism. Man's knowledge may not be "absolute," but it has no observable limits.
>
> That the academic world has managed to dismiss Steiner's works as inconsequential and irrelevant, is one of the intellectual wonders of the twentieth century.... Steiner was no more of a mystic than Albert Einstein; he was a scientist, rather—but a scientist who dared to enter into the mysteries of life.
>
> (Russell W. Davenport, *The Dignity of Man,* p.335)

Manfred Kyber[1] speaks of the issues to which I have addressed this

---

1. Author of *The Three Candles of Little Veronica.* Waldorf Press, Garden City, NY, 1975. *A New Humanity* is published in German: *Neues Menschentum,* Drei-Eichen Verlag, Engelberg, Switzerland, 1931.

book, and of the importance of Steiner's education to their solution, in the following passages from *A New Humanity:*

> The two fundamental mistakes of our Western civilization are its blind and almost most exclusive *worldliness,* on the one hand, and its *remoteness from nature,* on the other. When I speak of Western man, I mean the American as well as the European. America is faced with the same turning point in her civilization, although her crisis will presumably come at a later date. Asia may overcome this crisis because she has not yet become so detached from the spiritual and from nature as have Europe and America.

> Fostered for centuries, worldliness and remoteness from nature have dragged Western man down into an increasingly subhuman condition. They have broken his integrity and loosened his associations, so that he has become a creature who fumes and rages at himself. By subhuman we do not mean the animal part, for animals have remained within the framework of their essential nature. They have not risen so high nor sunk so low as have many human beings. The subhuman is equally far from the spiritual and from nature; it is far from both humanity and animality. *It is intelligence without feeling and spirit, speculation without intuition, an ego without spirituality....*

> Yet the thinking of our own Western world should not be condemned out of hand: It has examined the surface of existence as never before, and has developed the individualized, independent intelligence. Only at the expense of the connection with the other world could this achievement be made. Now, however, the task of materialism has been fulfilled. The understanding, now set free, must again associate itself with the spiritual world and not sink down into the subhuman as it is doing....

> Man has two natures, the worldly and the otherworldly, and we shall be able to solve the problems of mankind only when we find the synthesis of both in a spiritualized way of thinking. Even then we shall certainly not be infallible. We shall still make many

mistakes; but they will be human errors and hence such as can be put right again, not subhuman errors that lead into the blind alley we now face. In a spiritualized intelligence, thinking will again be coupled with morality without which *humanity* is inconceivable. Morality is a law of the next world, and as real there as is the force of gravity in this. Questions of mankind cannot be solved by any one-sided intelligence, but only by that eternally human element in all of us which is a synthesis of this world and the next....

In education, there have been so many attempts at reform that we may well hope to find at long last the correct way. Worldliness of thought and remoteness from nature, the two cardinal faults of Western civilization, must first of all be eliminated also from this sphere, where they have exerted their baleful influence for long enough.... As a general principle, it may be said of all systems of education that we need more cultivation of the thinking spirit and less knowledge and information. We must bring up good men and women who are full of life, not overloaded knowledge-boxes. This requires first and foremost a comprehension of the child as regards its true otherworldly nature.

In the first place, the suggestions given by Dr. Rudolf Steiner . . . to the teachers of the Free Waldorf School in Stuttgart here seem to me to be of great value. From supersensible intuition he has characterized the child's growth and development, and in all schools consideration should be given to Steiner's guiding principles.

APPENDIX B, PART 1

"Third Force" Psychology

The innumerable varieties of psychological doctrine today are generally grouped into three main streams: what we might call those of the left, the right, and the middle. In Maslow's words,

> The two comprehensive theories of human nature most influencing psychology until recently have been the Freudian and the experimental-positivistic-behavioristic. All other theories were less comprehensive and their adherents formed many splinter groups. In the last few years, however, these various groups have rapidly been coalescing into a third, increasingly comprehensive theory of human nature, into what might be called a "Third Force."[2]

Carl Rogers agrees that there are, indeed, three broad emphases in American psychology to which educators look for their ideas of human nature.

> These resemble three ocean currents flowing side by side, mingling, with no clear line of demarcation, yet definitely different.... Associated with the first trend are such terms as "behaviorism," "objective," "experimental," "impersonal," "logical-positivistic," "operational," "laboratory." Associated with the second current are terms such as "Freudian," "Neo-Freudian," "psychoanalytic," "psychology of the unconscious," "instinctual," "ego-psychology," "id-psychology," "dynamic psychology." Associated with the third are terms such as "phenomenological," "existential," "self-theory," "self-actualization," "health-and-growth psychology," "being and becoming," "science of inner experience."[3]

---

2. Abraham H. Maslow, *Toward a Psychology of Being,* New York, Van Nostrand Reinhold Company, 1968, p. ix.
3. Carl R. Rogers, "Toward a Science of the Person," in *Behaviorism and Phenomenology,* ed. T. W. Wann, Chicago, University of Chicago Press, 1964, p. 109.

"Each current in psychology," says Rogers, "has its own implicit philosophy of man."

> Though not often stated explicitly, these philosophies exert their influence in many significant and subtle ways. For the behaviorist, man is a machine, a complicated but nonetheless understandable machine, which we can learn to manipulate with greater and greater skill until he thinks the thoughts, moves in the directions, and behaves in the ways selected for him. For the Freudian, man is an irrational being, irrevocably in the grip of his past and of the product of that past, his unconscious.[4]

Ordinary folk are by now aware that Freud's concepts still exert a great influence on education. They also know a little something about the behavioristic theories. Perhaps they feel some dread of both, because the idea of man in both seems inhuman. Less well known is the many-faceted third force, the humanistic or self-psychology; but upon hearing of its purposes and its claims, one could believe that new champions of the human cause had at last appeared; one could hope that education is at last being offered a solid basis on which to build. Unfortunately, though this hope seems partly justified, it is far from being entirely so. Protestations notwithstanding, self-psychology, too, fails to grasp what is essential in the human being. It does not draw a clear line between what belongs to the truly self-determining spirit and what belongs to the genetically determined biological organism. The following excerpts from Abraham Maslow are offered in evidence.

> From the European writers, we can and should pick up their greater emphasis on what they call "philosophical anthropology," that is, the attempt to define man, and the differences between man and robots. What are his unique and defining characteristics? What is so essential to man that without it he would no longer be defined as a man?

---

4. *Ibid.*, p. 129.

On the whole this is a task from which American psychology has abdicated. The various behaviorisms don't generate any such definition, at least none that can be taken seriously (what *would* an S-R man be like? And who would like to be one?) Freud's picture of man was clearly unsuitable, leaving out as it did his aspirations, his realizable hopes, his godlike qualities.[5]

> ... human beings at their best are far more admirable (godlike, heroic, great, divine, awe-inspiring, lovable, etc.) than ever before conceived, in their *own* proper nature. There is no need to add a non-natural determinant to account for saintliness, heroism, altruism, transcendence, creativeness; etc.[6]

Maslow would persuade us that, in the case of man, a biological organism rises above itself yet remains self-identical. It confronts, opposes, subjugates, and refashions itself without being in any way other or more than itself.

> Transcendence ... means to become divine or godlike, to go beyond the merely human. But one must be careful ... not to make anything extra-human or supernatural of this kind of statement.[7]

> ... the highest experience ever described, the joyful fusion with the ultimate that man can conceive, can be seen simultaneously as the deepest experience of our ultimate personal animality and specieshood, as the acceptance of our profound biological nature as isomorphic with nature in general.... Communion by the person with that which transcends him can be seen as a biological experience.[8]

What all of this means is that the so-called spiritual or value-life, or "higher" life, is on the same continuum (is the same *kind* or

5. Maslow, *Toward a Psychology of Being*, p. 12.
6. Abraham H. Maslow, *Religions, Values, and Peak-Experiences,* New York, The Viking Press, 1964, p. 37.
7. Abraham H Maslow, *The Farther Reaches of Human Nature,* New York, The Viking Press, 1971, p. 272.
8. *Ibid.*, p. 334.

quality of thing) with the life of the flesh, or of the body, i.e., the animal life, the material life, the "lower" life. That is, the spiritual life is part of our biological life. It is the "highest" part of it, but yet part of it.

The spiritual life is then part of the human essence. It is a defining characteristic of human nature, without which human nature is not full human nature. It is part of the Real Self, of one's identity, of one's inner core, of one's specieshood of full humanness. . . .

The so-called spiritual (or transcendent, or axiological) life is clearly rooted in the biological nature of the species. It is a kind of "higher" animality whose precondition is a healthy "lower" animality.[9]

The lower animality of man has "basic" needs; the higher animality, in that it goes beyond the lower, has "metaneeds."

These metaneeds, though having certain special characteristics which differentiate them from basic needs, are yet in the same realm of discourse and of research as, for instance, the need for vitamin C or for calcium. They fall within the realm of science, broadly conceived, and are certainly *not* the exclusive property of theologians, philosophers or artists. The spiritual or value-life then falls well *within* the realm of nature rather than being a different and opposed realm. It is susceptible to investigation at once by psychologists and social scientists, and in theory will eventually become also a problem for neurology, endocrinology, genetics, and biochemistry as these sciences develop suitable methods.[10]

Since neurology, endocrinology and genetics as we know them are all forms of chemistry and physics, we should expect that moral-spiritual qualities such as pity, forgiveness, love, loyalty, honesty, and hope— as well as insight, understanding and wisdom, to say nothing of the

9. *Ibid.,* pp. 324-7.
10. *Ibid.,* p. 320.

creativeness of a Shakespeare, Raphael, and Beethoven—will all eventually be subjected to electro-chemical investigation and explanations.

> Basic-need and metaneed gratification help to make "better specimens," biological superiors, high in the dominance-hierarchy. Not only does the stronger, more dominant, more successful animal have more satisfactions, a better territory, more offspring, etc.—not only is the weaker animal lower in the dominance-hierarchy, more expendable, more likely to get eaten and less likely to reproduce, more likely to go hungry, etc., but the better specimen also lives a fuller life with more gratification and less frustration, pain, and fear.[11]

> From what we know of developments within individuals and within societies, a certain amount of spirituality is the extremely probable consequence of a satisfied materialism.[12]

Is it really so that Buddha, St. Francis of Assisi, Joan of Arc, were functioning as superior animals? Did their spirituality appear in consequence of a satisfied materialism? When Jesus of Nazareth received the Christ at the baptism in Jordan, and when the disciples received the Holy Spirit as recounted in Acts II: 4, were these, after all, really not a descent of the spirit *upon* human beings but a rising up of biological processes *within* them?

Let us follow Maslow further:

> . . . Man has a higher nature which is just as "instinctoid" as his lower nature. . . .[13]

> Since man's instinctoid tendencies, such as they are, are far weaker than cultural forces, it will always be a difficult task to tease out man's psychobiological values.[14]

---

11. Ibid, p 323.
12. *Ibid.*, p. 327.
13. *Toward a Psychology of Being*, p. 222.
14. *Ibid.*, p. 171.

An old-fashioned way of summarizing this is to say that man's higher nature rests upon man's lower nature, needing it as a foundation and collapsing without this foundation. That is, for the mass of mankind, man's higher nature is inconceivable without a satisfied lower nature as a base. The best way to develop this higher nature is to fulfill and gratify the lower nature first.[15]

The implication here is that man's higher nature, ideals, aspirations, and abilities rest not upon instinctual renunciation, but rather upon instinctual gratification. (Of course the "basic needs" I've been talking about are not the same as the "instincts" of the classical Freudians.)[16]

Maslow was serious about raising the higher out of the lower; and, of course, when human development is viewed from the outside, this is truly what happens. Even the sage, saint, or hero, if looked at externally, appears as no more than a body engaged in certain behaviors. Paul, after Damascus, seemed the same body as Saul before Damascus. The body simply changed its way of behaving. But how and why did it change? Can such a question concerning human actions be answered from outside, or do we not have to ask the person involved? Paul himself gives no possible support for the idea that his transformation was simply the rising up of next higher instincts in him out of lower instincts that had been gratified.

APPENDIX B, PART 2

Maslow on Values

The following quotations from Abraham Maslow's *Toward a Psychology of Being* indicate that the ethical views developed by Kelley and Rasey from the science available to them have not been outmoded by

---

15. *Ibid.*, p. 173.
16. *Ibid.*, p. 179.

recent developments among the more humanistic psychologists. The knowledge of good and evil, right and wrong, honorable and dishonorable, is still thought to be given to us by our organism.

> . . . ultimately the search for identity, is, in essence, the search for one's own intrinsic authentic values. (p. 177)

> It appears to me that these values . . . are intrinsic in the structure of human nature itself, that they are biologically and genetically based, as well as culturally developed . . . (p. 167)

> My thesis is then: that we can, in principle, have a descriptive, naturalistic science of human values; that the age-old mutually exclusive contrast between "what is" and "what ought to be" is in part a false one; that we can study the highest values or goals of human beings as we study the values of ants or horses or oak trees, or, for that matter, Martians. We can discover (rather than create or invent) which values men trend toward, yearn for, struggle for, as they improve themselves, and which values they lose as they get sick. (p. 167)

> Observe that if these assumptions are proven true, they promise a scientific ethics, a natural value system, a court of ultimate appeal for the determination of good and bad, of right and wrong.... This amounts to automatic solution of many of the personality problems of the future. The thing to do seems to be to find out what one is *really* like inside, deep down, as a member of the human species and as a particular individual. (p. 4)

> All this implies a naturalistic system of values, a by-product of the empirical description of the deepest tendencies of the human species and of specific individuals. The study of the human being by science or by self-search can discover where he is heading What is his purpose in life, what is good for him and what is bad for him, what will make him feel virtuous and what will make him feel guilty, why choosing the good is often difficult for him, what the attractions of evil are. (Observe that the word "ought" need not be used. . . .) (p. 205)

There is no doubt that human values or ethics can be studied, *after* people have made them their own. By then they have become historical facts, whose evolutionary appearance, meaning, benefits for life, relationships to the values of other human beings, and so on, may well be examined. But until one has said to a particular ethical idea, "I, John Brown, being of sound mind and acting of my own will, do testify herewith that I mean to adopt and identify myself with you; my freely conceived hope is that I may be strong enough to follow you through thick and thin"—the idea is not yet, properly speaking, *one's own*. At best, it is no more than a suggestion offered by the voice of one's conscience. But conscience is rightly said to speak with the stillest and smallest of voices, while the powers against which it speaks have no such reticence: anger, fear, hate, and desire speak imperiously. They have instinctive power; they do not hesitate to wield it for all they are worth; if they can move a person, they certainly will. That the ethical values voiced by conscience, however, are not instincts, is clear from the fact that in our time they have no real power to persuade. They are no more instinctive than any other objective truth, such as a geometrical theorem or a formula in physics. They state the objective case briefly, and retire. If people move to take them for their own, that is their affair; just as if they choose to *apply* geometry or physics in their lives. But such people will walk every step of the way by their *own* effort, not induced or compelled by conscience. Were the intuition of ethical concepts instinctive, we would not be so free in the first place to neglect making such intuitions, and in the second place to fail of following them.

The comparison of ethical with mathematical or scientific intuitions supports Maslow when he says that we can "discover" ethical values. Such values exist as ideal possibilities, and we can seek to discover which of them will effect what we wish to bring out of a given situation. But no matter what ideas we find, they will not become actual *values* until we choose to value them, being perfectly clear at that time about what it is we are choosing. Nothing will come of ethical ideas, unless we persist by our own force in *making them* operative as values in our world. In that event, we shall realize that in every instance of moral choice we are creating, not merely discovering. We shall also know very well that by and through this uncompelled, original, creative choice and enactment, it is not only ethical values we are bringing into existence, but ourselves. If we cannot be *creative* of our own values, we cannot really cause our own actions. But insofar as human beings are not the absolute authors of their own behavior, their individualities are cancelled. Strictly speaking, such people do not exist. This is a strange view for a leader of "existential," "humanistic," "being" psychology to propose.

Ethical values are not "deep down" in the organism of a person. As ideas, they are of the substance of the all-pervading, all-encompassing world-spirit. They become human values only for those who identify themselves with this spirit, making of its concepts their own wills. Such people, in order to come to this insightful deed must ask of their organisms that they hold back from exerting any influence at all. The fact suggested by Maslow—that, all things being equal, the organisms of ethical people will prosper—has nothing to do with the intrinsic content of their ethical ideas nor with the moment when such people convert them to active values. Genuine scientists choose their ideas not because those ideas promise profit, but because they are true. Genuine artists choose beauty not for the sake of their own health but for beauty's own sake. Genuinely moral people adopt ethical ideas not because it will favor them or their organisms, but because they find ethics and goodness inherently lovable.

APPENDIX C, PART 1

A Further Comment on the Human Being as Organism

Education and the Nature of Man impressed me when I first read it long ago, because it tried to make a single, simple picture out of what various scientific disciplines were agreeing upon as up-to-date knowledge of humanity, and it tried to state plainly the implications of this picture for the education of human beings. The book was the popularized science, what has been called the scientism, of that time. Yet the basic idea of human nature that Kelley and Rasey put forward is still in vogue. For the leaders of educational thought, the human being is still, perhaps more than ever, an organism with "tissue purposes" and all the rest. They still allege that thinking is done by the brain—not by human beings themselves with or through their brains. For them, thought only seems to be thought; for clinicians, thought is the work of organic habits, instincts, and drives; for laboratory technicians, it is electro-chemical circuits and transactions among the cerebral neurons.

As evidence of bio-physical and bio-chemical views of the nature of human thinking, I quote without comment (though the titles are mine) from a small booklet called *Discovering Yourself in the Brain Age*, published by the National Institute of Neurological & Communicative Disorders & Stroke of the Department of Health, Education, and Welfare (DHEW Publication No. (NIH) 72-330). This booklet, printed in 1973, is for sale by the Superintendent of Documents, U.S. Government Printing Office. It was strongly recommended by a letter of November, 1974, to all science teachers in the United States.

Who Am I Really?

Think about yourself. Do you feel like a "thing," living in a world of "things?". . . if we ignore the process-character of reality and try to live in a rigid world of "things," we are headed for trouble—for *things they are a-changing!* And that is what life and science are all about. (p. 2)

The meaning of the "search for identity," the search to find out "who in fact you are," is often misunderstood.... What we mean by man's quest to find out *who he is* might be better understood as an attempt to discover more fully *what he is,* or what he is becoming. In other words, many people feel the need to experience a deeper sense of what their organisms are doing in the world. (p. 5)

What you "are" is changing all the time.... We can declare that a particular man is an electrician, a husband, a father and a citizen, but if we are even to begin to understand what he *is,* we need to see him as a unique and dynamic combination of cells, organs, enzymes, hormones, electrochemical interactions, and much more.

You may seem the same to others from day to day, but beneath the appearance of stability you present are the biological rhythms, the hormonal tides, the building up and breaking down of cells, the rise and fall of enzyme activities, the constant surgings of nerve impulses and neuronal waves....

To discover what or "who" you are means to learn to take more and more of the reality of yourself into account.... All ... aspects of yourself are centered in the functioning of your brain. When you ask "who am I," perhaps the most profound answer you could receive is that you are all of the complex processes of your brain. You may sense that your "self" is like a little man hiding somewhere inside your head, separate from the wrinkled jelly and neuronal network that is also there. It takes a further jump of the imagination to realize that as far as anyone knows the "self" is precisely that vastly complex neurological machine called your brain and nervous system. (pp. 6-7)

What About Individuality?

We can begin to appreciate our uniqueness better when we gain a greater understanding of why no two people's experiences are ever exactly the same. We each start out with a personal bias built into us through our genetic inheritance, and throughout our lives we attend to the world selectively from moment to moment according to our personal biological rhythms and the complex needs of our organism. And watching over it all is the brain....

The trick has been for the brain to become sufficiently aware of its own significance to allow itself to be investigated by its own scientific method. The trick for you can be to learn to imagine yourself as the process/brain (your brain/ self), and to see others as their process-selves. (pp. 10-11)

What About Spiritual Life? What About Thought?

All the elaborate mental images and conceptions which you ordinarily think of as your "ideas," "opinions," "thoughts," or "knowledge," appear to exist as complex arrangements of electrical/chemical activity in these areas of the new brain. . . .

. . . the billions of cells in your association areas carry electrical/ chemical charges which account for your "mental state.". . . the possibility of electrical exchange is vast. These exchanges, or you might say "thoughts," that actually occur depend a great deal on the relative chemical states of the various cells through time. Your thought patterns . . . seem to be the result of paths formed chemically among the cells. . . . All of your awareness, values, beliefs, and memories appear objectively to be patterns of electrical impulses maintained through the chemicals of your brain cells. . . . Your old brain would seem to be the source of your "instinctual" urges, such as to find a mate, to establish a home, to hunt for resources, to breed and to defend your territory . . . such qualities of mind as empathy, humane understanding and compassion grow out of the proper integration of the old brain with the new brain. (pp. 16-17)

Do I Decide, or Does my Brain?

Your limbic brain is intimately involved in directing your sexual and emotional behavior, and it functions to integrate information coming to the brain from inside and outside of your body. It is apparently continuously bombarded by impulses from your internal environment, which it processes so as to provide the new brain and the rest of your organism with an "interpretation" upon which your organism can act.

This "interpretation" might be considered that which makes you unique, the built-in bias asserted from moment-to-moment by your organism, the crucial physiological function that makes you you. (p. 18)

. . . the limbic brain also has the capacity to stimulate feelings in you about what is true, real or important. Your limbic brain may be responsible for the experience described as "exercising your free will." (p. 18)

. . . what seems to be a decisive act of will may result from the ability of your limbic brain to *anticipate* the attitude of your organism toward a plan of action proposed by your new brain. If this is what happens, then it may not be a matter of your making a "decision," so much as your limbic brain telling your new brain how the rest of your organism feels about the idea. The "freedom" which at first seems so apparent could turn out to be just a trick of perception by which the nervous system lets the new brain know in advance what the whole organism is bound and determined to do. (p. 19)

APPENDIX C, PART 2

Skinner on the Autonomous Human Being

While our attention has been focused on Third-force psychologists, since these claim to take more account of the complete nature of man than do Freudians or behaviorists, one or another kind of behaviorism tends to dominate educational psychology at the present time. The reader may wish to compare, through the following quotations, the idea of man developed in Skinner's form of behaviorism with that put forward by Maslow's humanism. Skinner writes:

Matson has argued that "the empirical behavioral scientist . . . denies, if only by implication, that a unique being, called Man, exists." "What is now under attack," said Maslow, "is the 'being' of man." C. S. Lewis put it quite bluntly: Man is being abolished.
(*Beyond Freedom and Dignity,* p. 200)

We are told that what is threatened is "man *qua* man," or "man in his humanity," or "man as Thou not It," or "man as a person not a thing." These are not very helpful expressions, but they supply a clue. What is being abolished is autonomous man—the inner man, the homunculus, the possessing demon, the person defended by the literatures of freedom and dignity.

His abolition has long been overdue. The autonomous man is a device used to explain what we cannot explain in any other way. He has been constructed from his ignorance, and as his understanding increases, the very stuff of which he is composed vanishes. (p. 200)

Krutch has argued that whereas the traditional view supports Hamlet's exclamation, "How like a god!" Pavlov, the behavioral scientist, emphasized "How like a dog!" But that was a step forward. A god is the archetypal pattern of an explanatory fiction, of a miracle-working mind, of the metaphysical. (p. 201)

The function of the inner man is to provide an explanation which will not be explained in turn. Explanation stops with him He is not a mediator between past history and current behavior; he is a *center* from which behavior emanates. He initiates, originates, and creates, and in doing so he remains, as he was for the Greeks, divine. We say that he is autonomous—and, so far as a science of behavior is concerned, that means miraculous.

The position is of course, vulnerable. Autonomous man serves to explain only the things we are not yet able to explain in other ways. His existence depends upon our ignorance, and he naturally loses status as we come to know more about behavior. (p. 14)

As a science of behavior adopts the strategy of physics and biology the autonomous agent to which behavior has traditionally been attributed is replaced by the environment. (p. 186)

Regardless of any normal genetic endowment, an organism will range between vigorous activity and complete quiescence depending upon the schedules on which it has been reinforced. (p. 186)

The inner gatekeeper is replaced by the contingencies to which the organism has been exposed and which select the stimuli to which it reacts. (p. 187)

Whatever we do, and hence however we perceive it, the fact remains that it is the environment which acts upon the perceiving person, not the perceiving person who acts upon the environment. (p. 188)

A scientific analysis of behavior dispossesses autonomous man and turns the control he has been said to exert to the environment. (p. 205)

In shifting control from autonomous man to the observable environment we do not leave an empty organism. A great deal goes on inside the skin, and physiology will eventually tell us more about it. (p. 195)

Personal exemption from a complete determinism is revoked as a scientific analysis progresses, particularly in accounting for the behavior of the individual. (p. 21)

The picture which emerges from a scientific analysis is not of a body with a person inside, but of a body which *is* a person in the sense that it displays a complex repertoire of behavior. (p. 199)

Man is a machine in the sense that he is a complex system behaving in lawful ways, but the complexity is extraordinary. (p. 202)

It is in the nature of an experimental analysis of human behavior that it should strip away the functions previously assigned to autonomous man and transfer them one by one to the controlling environment. The analysis leaves less and less for autonomous man to do. But what about man himself? Is there not something about a person which is more than a living body? Unless something called a self survives, how can we speak of self-knowledge or self-control? To whom is the injunction "Know thyself" addressed? (p. 198)

A self is a repertoire of behavior appropriate to a given set of contingencies.... Two or more repertoires generated by different sets of contingencies compose two or more selves. (p. 199)

... the individual is at best a locus in which many lines of development come together in a unique set. His individuality is unquestioned. Every cell in his body is a unique genetic product, as unique as that classic mark of individuality, the fingerprint. And even within the most regimented culture every personal history is unique. (p. 209)

Is man then "abolished?" Certainly not as a species or as an individual achiever. It is the autonomous inner man who is abolished, and that is a step forward. (p. 215)

Perhaps the last stronghold of autonomous man is that complex "cognitive" activity called thinking. Because it is complex, it has yielded only slowly to explanation in terms of contingencies of reinforcement. (p. 193)

Abstract thinking is the product of a particular kind of environment, not of a cognitive faculty. (p. 189)

It is not hard to understand why Skinner's concept of human cognition would lead him to programmed learning and teaching machines.

Skinner is more outspoken in his dismissal of the allegedly autonomous being called the human spirit than is Maslow; but do they really differ, when all is said and done?

Third-force psychology attempts to build a monistic world conception upon the wondrous properties of matter. It sees metaphysical, transcendent, "godlike" experiences as delightful vapors that float up from the depths of our material organism. But what becomes of these godlike experiences; what becomes of the human individuality at death? Death is the moment of truth for any philosophy of life. Materialistic monisms speak bravely of "spiritual" experiences, but can this spirit pass the ultimate test? Obviously not, since when the material foundation crumbles, the whole superstructure comes tumbling down. Death tests mere words against reality. Death decides between Christ's achieved statement, "Ye are in the world *but not of it*" and Maslow's wishful thinking that "one can transcend the universe of time and space *while being of it."* [Emphasis supplied.] *(Religions, Values, and Peak Experiences,* p. 116)

The idealistic humanism of such psychologists as Abraham Maslow and Erich Fromm speaks as highly as possible of human integrity, power of choice, depth of experience, and creative potentiality; but death decides between rhetoric and reality. "Man's life," says Fromm in *Man for Himself,*

> beginning and ending at one accidental point in the evolutionary process of the race, conflicts tragically with the individual's claim for the realization of all of his potentialities.... There is only one solution to his problem: to face the truth, to acknowledge his fundamental aloneness and solitude in a universe indifferent to his fate, to recognize that there is no power transcending him which can solve his problem for him. Man must accept the responsibility for himself and the fact that only by using his own powers can he give meaning to his life. (pp. 43-5)

We must admire the courage involved in this existential statement and can agree with it that mature individuals accept full responsibility for their own behavior and feel ready and able to set their own goals for themselves. But the actual experience of such freedom carries with it a conviction, a certitude, that Fromm either cannot see or will not state. People who have come to the stage of self-determination do not ask anyone else to take charge of their moral condition, or to preserve them in eternity in an immoral state. What they do come to perceive with certainty, however, is that the eternal that wakes in them during physical life on Earth, growing stronger and stronger in the mastery of life through cognition, love, and creativeness, is self-subsistent. Because it rests on nothing other than itself, it has no part in the body's decay. This eternal knows itself to be surrounded and transfused by other eternal being.

Maslow is somewhat more sentimental, more evasive, about death than Fromm; but the implications of his view are clear enough. He has this to say:

> Perhaps I should add here the paradoxical result—for some— that death may lose its dread aspect. Ecstasy is somehow close to death-experience, at least in the simple, empirical sense that death is often mentioned during reports of peaks, sweet death that is. After the acme, only less is possible. In any case, I have occasionally been told, "I felt that I could willingly die," or "No one can ever again tell me death is bad," etc. Experiencing a kind of "sweet death" may remove its frightening aspect. (*Religions, Values, and Peak Experiences*, p. 76)

> Older people, making their peace with death, are more apt to be profoundly touched, with (sweet) sadness and tears at the contrast between their own mortality and the eternal quality of what sets off the experience. This contrast can make far more poignant and precious what is being witnessed, e.g., "The surf will be here forever and you will soon be gone. So hang on to it; appreciate it; be fully conscious of it. Be grateful for it. You are lucky." (*The Farther Reaches of Human Nature*, p. 348)

Skinner, who from the beginning dispensed with the pseudo-autonomous human being that still haunts humanistic psychologists, is at least self-consistent about the prospect facing the individual human being and all humanity:

> "The limits of perfection of the human species," said Etienne Cabet in *Voyage en Icarie*, "are as yet unknown." But, of course, there are no limits. The human species will never reach a final state of perfection before it is exterminated— "some say in fire, some in ice," and some in radiation. (*Beyond Freedom and Dignity*, p. 208)

APPENDIX C, PART 3

The Use of Drugs

In trying to evaluate Maslow's humanism, one can call upon logic, or upon history, for confirmatory or negative evidence. But one can also ask the pragmatic question: What difference does it make whether psychology sees spiritual life as something self-subsistent and self-determining, or as simply a kind of delicate bodily process? No doubt, many books would need to be written, should a thorough answer to this question be attempted. But there is one answer that can be suggested quite briefly. Whoever imagines that spiritual life is evoked from the body will incline to favor experimental manipulation of the body, hoping to discover thereby which medical treatment will induce the body to bring forth its spiritual treasures. Young people today who experience spiritual longing yet cannot free themselves from the materialistic interpretation of life to which they have been educated, are seeking the higher life through sex and drugs and diet. Though Maslow saw clearly enough that this kind of quest *could* lead to trouble, fundamentally he favored it. His road map to spiritual experience did not advise the young to subdue the body by focusing clear consciousness, but by the unfocusing of rational consciousness to let the body come forward with its inclinations and intimations. He did not counsel intensive absorption into objective thoughts or observations (subordinating one's own promptings) so that *their* lives could at the same time be their own higher lives; but he recommended abandoning both conscious self-possession and objective cognition of the world, in order that dim subjective voices, hints from the animal nature within, might be heard. To this end, he felt, drugs might be helpful.

The American humanistic psychologists and existential psychiatrists . . . conceive of the human being as having an essence, a biological nature, membership in a species. It is very easy to interpret the "uncovering" therapies as helping the person to *discover* his Identity, his Real Self, in a word, his own subjective biology, which he can *then* proceed to actualize, to "make himself," to "choose."

The trouble is that the human species is the only species which finds it hard to be a species. For a cat there seems to be no problem about being a cat. It's easy; cats seem to have no complexes or ambivalences or conflicts, and show no signs of yearning to be dogs instead. Their instincts are very clear. But *we* have no such unequivocal animal instincts. Our biological essence, our instinct remnants, are weak and subtle, and they are hard to get at.... These deepest impulses in the human species, at the points where the instincts have been lost almost entirely, where they are extremely weak, extremely subtle and delicate, where you have to dig to find them, *this is* where I speak of introspective biology, of biological phenomenology, implying that one of the necessary methods in the search for identity, the search for self, the search for spontaneity and for naturalness is a matter of closing your eyes, cutting down the noise, turning off the thoughts, putting away all busyness, just relaxing in a kind of Taoistic and receptive fashion (in much the same way that you do on the psychoanalyst's couch). The technique here is to just wait to see what happens, what comes to mind. This is what Freud called free association, free-floating attention rather than task orientation, and if you are successful in this effort and learn how to do it, you can forget about the outside world and its noises and begin to hear these small, delicate impulse voices from within, the hints from your animal nature, not only from your common species-nature, but also from your own uniqueness. (*The Farther Reaches of Human Nature,* p. 186)

In the last few years it has become quite clear that certain drugs called "psychedelic," especially LSD and psilocybin, give us some possibility of control in this realm of peak-experiences. It looks as if these drugs often produce peak-experiences in the right people under the right circumstances, so that perhaps we needn't wait for them to occur by good fortune. Perhaps we can actually produce a private personal peak-experience under observation and whenever we wish under religious or non-religious circumstances. We may then be able to study in its moment of birth the experience of illumination or revelation. Even more important, it may be that these drugs and perhaps also hypnosis, could be used to produce a peak-experience, with core-religious revelation, in non-peakers, thus bridging the chasm between these too separated halves of mankind. (*Religions, Values, and Peak-Experiences*, p. 27)

For instance, in using psychedelic drugs to produce peak-experiences, general experience has been that if the atmosphere is coldly clinical or investigatory, and if the subject is watched and studied as if with a microscope, like a bug on a pin, then peaks are less apt to occur and unhappy experiences are more apt to occur. When the atmosphere becomes one of brotherly communion, however, with perhaps one of the 'investigator-brothers' himself also taking the drug, then the experience is much more likely to be ecstatic and transcendent. (*Religions, Values, and Peak-Experiences*, p. 87)

Reasoning thus, Maslow did not appreciate the unlifelikeness of his conclusion; for though a pill can make a person *feel* strong, it builds no actual muscle. One can believe, indeed, that it is actually destroying tissue when it manages to release the illusion of strength. Is it otherwise with the drugs that release mystic experiences? Do they really strengthen the spirit, or do they by their conjuring weaken it, rather, and the body too? One can well believe that the bodily organism, together with all else in the natural cosmos, is ultimately spiritual, its materiality being but the way in which spiritual workings appear to external observation. One can believe that a drug has power to derange both organic processes and consciousness, so that they penetrate each other, so that consciousness receives hints of the marvels that really underlie the body. But how is the one who has abandoned clarity of mind to distinguish truth from illusion; how is the one who has left self-possession behind to be master of his or her responses? There are clean and unclean spirits. There are spirits of ugliness as well as of beauty. The only spirit that speaks for the true essence of a person's own being utters itself in the *I am*. This power is sabotaged by any influence that dims or splits clarity of observation and thinking. The power of the I am is strengthened only by one's own efforts to be absolutely on target, and clear, and loving withal.

In the 1973 booklet of the Department of Health, Education and Welfare already referred to, appears an additional statement concerning the use of drugs to regulate the mind.

> Imagine the time when doctors may cure brain dysfunctions routinely by making minute electrical or chemical changes in a patient's brain cells.... Consider the prospect of taking "learning pills" as an aid to learning French or algebra. Or the psychopathic killer who may be changed into a normally functioning person through alteration of a few malfunctioning brain cells.... "We are just on the threshold. And where we will go—I don't know. But it is so far, so fast, that our wildest dreams are likely to be ultra-conservative." (p. 26)

> ... brain scientists feel the physician has a role in diagnosing and treating violent individuals.... Scientists feel knowledge about the brain functions in violent persons with brain disease can be used to favorably influence the violence-triggering mechanisms in the brains of non-diseased, but violent, individuals. (pp. 28-29)
> Surgery is a method of treatment....
> Electrical stimulation of the brain (ESB) has been used for many years....
> We often hear of drugs in frightening contexts, and indeed the fruits of research of all kinds can be abused. But ... even LSD, the dread potion which has been subject to so many frightening headlines in recent years, may find respectability through well-controlled research. (pp. 29-30)

Is it not reasonable to suppose that if the cure for non-diseased but violent persons is to be achieved through delicate brain surgery or through drugs, in future our society, in its concern for the "general welfare," or for the implementation of certain political or economic ends, could solve in the same way many other problems of a kind formerly called educational and ethical? Will discontent and rebelliousness, the tendency to intuitive experience, illusions of the soul and spirit, also be detected as early as possible, and eliminated, at the same time violence is being taken care of?

APPENDIX D, PART 1

Skinner on Education as Conditioning, as External Control of Behavior

Despite the difficulty of B. F. Skinner's technical language, some may find this rather extensive sample of his reasoning about the scientific manipulation of human behavior worth studying carefully for its far-reaching implications. In many ways, his views express the dominant trend of educational thinking in America today.

> If we are to use the methods of science in the field of human affairs, we must assume that behavior is lawful and determined. We must expect to discover that what a man does is the result of specifiable conditions and that once these conditions have been discovered, we can anticipate and to some extent determine his actions.
>
> This possibility is offensive to many people. It is opposed to a tradition of long standing which regards man as a free agent, whose behavior is the product, not of specifiable antecedent conditions, but of spontaneous inner changes of course. Prevailing philosophies of human nature recognize an internal "will" which makes the prediction and control of behavior impossible. To suggest that we abandon this view is to threaten many cherished beliefs. . . . The alternative point of view insists upon recognizing coercive forces in human conduct which we may prefer to disregard. It challenges our aspirations, either worldly or otherwordly. (pp. 6-7)

> Primitive beliefs about man and his place in nature are usually flattering. It has been the unfortunate responsibility of science to paint more realistic pictures. The Copernican theory of the solar system displaced man from his preeminent position at the center of things. Today we accept this theory without emotion, but originally it met with enormous resistance. Darwin challenged a practice of segregation in which man set himself firmly apart from the animals, and the bitter struggle which arose is not yet ended. But though Darwin put man in his biological place, he did not deny

him a possible position as master. Special faculties or a special capacity for spontaneous, creative action might have emerged in the process of evolution. When that distinction is now questioned, a new threat arises.

There are many ways of hedging on the theoretical issue. It may be insisted that a science of human behavior is impossible, that behavior has certain essential features which forever keep it beyond the pale of science. But although this argument may dissuade many people from further inquiry, it is not likely to have any effect upon those who are willing to try and see. (pp. 7-8)

All this suggests that we are in transition. We have not wholly abandoned the traditional philosophy of human nature; at the same time we are far from adopting a scientific point of view without reservation. We have accepted the assumption of determinism in part; yet we allow our sympathies, our first allegiances, and our personal aspirations to rise to the defense of the traditional view. We are currently engaged in a sort of patchwork in which new facts and methods are assembled in accordance with traditional theories.

If this were a theoretical issue only, we would have no cause for alarm; but theories affect practices. A scientific conception of human behavior dictates one practice, a philosophy of personal freedom another. Confusion in theory means confusion in practice. The present unhappy condition of the world may in large measure be traced to our vacillation. The principal issues in dispute between nations, both in peaceful assembly and on the battlefield, are intimately concerned with the problem of human freedom and control. (p. 9)

. . . . .

The external variables of which behavior is a function provide for what may be called a causal or functional analysis. We undertake to predict and control the behavior of the individual organism. This is our "dependent variable"—the effect for which we are to find the cause. Our "independent variables"—the causes of behavior—are the external conditions of which behavior is a function.

Relations between the two—the "cause-and-effect relationships" in behavior—are the laws of a science. A synthesis of these laws expressed in quantitative terms yields a comprehensive picture of the organism as a behaving system. (p. 35)

It could be rash to assert at this point that there is no essential difference between human behavior and the behavior of lower species; but until an attempt has been made to deal with both in the same terms, it would be equally rash to assert that there is. (p. 38)

In the present analysis we cannot distinguish between involuntary and voluntary behavior by raising the issue of who is in control. It does not matter whether behavior is due to a willing individual or a psychic usurper, if we dismiss all inner agents of whatever sort. Nor can we make the distinction on the basis of control or lack of control, since we assume that no behavior is free. If we have no reason to distinguish between being able to do something and doing it, such expressions as "not being able to do something" or "not being able to help doing something" must be interpreted in some other way. When all relevant variables have been arranged, an organism will or will not respond. If it does not, it cannot. If it can, it will. (pp. 111-112)

The distinction between voluntary and involuntary behavior is a matter of the *kind* of control. It corresponds to the distinction between eliciting and discriminative stimuli. The eliciting stimulus appears to be coercive. Its causal connection with behavior is relatively simple and easily observed. This may explain why it was discovered first. The discriminative stimulus, on the other hand, shares its control with other variables, so that the inevitability of its effect cannot be easily demonstrated. But when all relevant variables have been taken into account, it is not difficult to guarantee the result—to force the discriminative operant as inexorably as the eliciting stimulus forces its response. (p. 112)

Implicit in a functional analysis is the notion of control. When we discover an independent variable which can be controlled, we discover a means of controlling the behavior which is a function of it. This fact is important for theoretical purposes. . . . The practical implications are probably even greater. An analysis of the techniques through which behavior may be manipulated shows the kind of technology which is emerging as the science advances, and it points up the considerable degree of control which is currently exerted. The problems raised by the control of human behavior obviously can no longer be avoided by refusing to recognize the possibility of control. (p. 227)

. . . . .

When a man controls himself, chooses a course of action, thinks out the solution to a problem or strives toward an increase in self-knowledge, he is *behaving.* He controls himself precisely as he would control the behavior of anyone else—through the manipulation of variables of which behavior is a function. His behavior in so doing is a proper object of analysis, and eventually it must be accounted for with variables lying *outside* the individual himself. (pp. 228-229)

A man may spend a great deal of time designing his own life—may choose the circumstances in which he is to live with great care, and he may manipulate his daily environment on an extensive scale. Such activity appears to exemplify a high order of self-determination. But it is also behavior, and we account for it in terms of other variables in the environment and history of the individual. It is these variables which provide the ultimate control.

This view is, of course, in conflict with traditional treatments of the subject, which are especially likely to cite self-control as an important example of the operation of personal responsibility. But an analysis which appeals to external variables makes the assumption of an inner originating and determining agent unnecessary. The scientific advantages of such an analysis are many, but the practical advantages may well be even more important. The traditional conception of what is happening when an individual controls himself has never been successful as an educational device.... An alternative analysis of the *behavior* of control should make it possible to teach relevant techniques as easily as any other technical repertoire. It should also improve the procedures through which society maintains self-controlling behavior in strength. (pp. 240-241)

The result of solving a problem is the appearance of a solution in the form of a response. The response alters the situation so that the problem disappears. The relation between the preliminary behavior and the appearance of the solution is simply the relation between the manipulation of variables and the emission of a response. Until the functional relations in behavior had been analyzed, this could not be clearly understood, and meanwhile a great many fictional processes were invented. Conspicuous examples are the "thought process" called thinking and reasoning. A functional analysis removes much of the mystery which surrounds these terms. We need not ask, for example, "where a solution comes from." A solution is a response which exists in some strength in the repertoire of the individual, if the problem is soluble by him. The appearance of the response in his behavior is no more surprising than the appearance of any response in the behavior of any organism. It is either meaningless or idle to ask where the response resides until it summons strength enough to spring out into the open. (p. 252)

. . . . .

We saw that self-control rests ultimately with the environmental variables which generate controlling behavior and, therefore, originates outside the organism. There is a parallel issue in the field of ideas. Is an idea ever original? . . . Man is now in much better control of the world than were his ancestors, and this suggests a progress in discovery and invention in which there appears to be a strong element of originality. But we could express this fact just as well by saying that the environment is now in better control of man. Reinforcing contingencies shape the behavior of the individual, and novel contingencies generate novel forms of behavior. Here, if anywhere, originality is to be found. . . . Educational agencies established by the group provide for the transmission of the results of environmental contingencies from one individual to another, and it becomes possible for the individual to acquire effective behavior on a vast scale. (pp. 254-255)

What is meant by the "self" in self-control or self-knowledge? . . . The self is most commonly used as a hypothetical cause of action. So long as external variables go unnoticed or are ignored, their function is assigned to an originating agent within the organism. If we cannot show what is responsible for a man's behavior, we say that he himself is responsible for it. The precursors of physical science once followed the same practices but the wind is no longer blown by Aeolus, nor is the rain cast down by Jupiter Pluvius. (p. 283)

. . . . .

Education is the establishing of behavior which will be of advantage to the individual and to others at some future time. The behavior will eventually he reinforced in many of the ways we have already considered; meanwhile reinforcements are arranged by the educational agency for the purpose of conditioning. (p.402)

A child is sent to a particular school largely because of what the school will teach. Those who are in ultimate control—for example, those who supply the institution with money—may insist that the curriculum be closely followed. The college supported by a religious agency engages in appropriate religious instruction and must not establish behavior opposed to the interests of the agency. Schools supported by a government may be asked to apply their educational techniques in supporting the government and to avoid any education which conflicts with governmental techniques of control or threatens the sources of governmental power.

Since other types of agencies also engage in educational control, they often enlist the services of the educational institution. Economic and religious agencies sometimes supply materials for school use which encourage education in line with economic or religious control. It may be necessary for a governmental agency to restrict the extent to which public schools serve other agencies in this way. (pp. 411-412)

. . . . .

A rigorous science of behavior makes a different sort of remote consequence effective when it leads us to recognize survival as a criterion in evaluating a controlling practice. We have seen that happiness, justice, knowledge, and so on are not far removed from certain immediate consequences which reinforce the individual in selecting one culture or one practice against another. But just as the immediate advantage gained through punishment is eventually matched by later disadvantages, these immediate consequences of a cultural practice may be followed by others of a different sort. A scientific analysis may lead us to resist the more immediate banishments of freedom, justice, knowledge, or happiness in considering the long-run consequence of survival. (pp. 435-436)

The hypothesis that man is not free is essential to the application of scientific method to the study of human behavior. The free inner man who is held responsible for the behavior of the external biological organism is only a pre-scientific substitute for the kinds of causes which are discovered in the course of a scientific analysis. (p. 447)

If science does not confirm the assumptions of freedom, initiative, and responsibility in the behavior of the individual, these assumptions will not ultimately be effective either as motivating devices or as goals in the design of culture. We may not give them up easily, and we may, in fact, find it difficult to control ourselves or others until alternative principles have been developed. But the change will probably be made. (p. 449)

—*Science and Human Behavior*

APPENDIX D, PART 2

Programmed Learning
(Article by John F. Gardner, reprinted from *Education as an Art*,
Summer, 1969)

Years ago I was asked to give my teacher's reaction to the concept of
"programmed" learning, or teaching, as put forward by behavioristic
psychologists. What follows is that brief statement, very slightly revised.

. . . . .

The difference between the text of programmed instruction and the
drama of real teaching is the difference between death and life. For society and the natural kingdoms of the earth that support human society, one cannot exaggerate the difference it makes whether students
are deadened or enlivened by the education we give them.

Programs are based on logical analysis. They suppose that any subject is composed of factual parts, that these parts are related to one another in a logical way, and that systematic presentation will therefore
succeed in conveying the truth of a matter. Such programs are certainly possible, and they do convey information. But their information
falls short of truth. It is of a mechanical nature. When the logical parts
of a program are put together, the machine-like result is related to integral truth as a corpse is related to the previously living body.

No assemblage of limbs and organs ever adds up to a living body.
No merely logical presentation of "facts" will conjure up the active
unity, the integrity, of bird or flower, of landscape or social group.
Unless and until programmed instruction is written as full-fledged
art—as poem, drama and story, really—seeking to convey in every
phrase the pulse of life, students will be receiving stones instead of
bread. Atomism and materialism will come to obsess their minds.
They will have been set by schooling itself upon the road that leads
in the end to decay and despair. At the least, they will become dry in
the joints and prosaic in the mind, boring to others as well as to
themselves.

The augury for the civilization that confides any major part of the
task of education to programs and teaching machines is bleak.

There may be a time for methodical analysis, even to the point of dissecting corpses, even to the point of learning from life-process how to make better machines. But is that time childhood and youth, when all should be growth and becoming? Perhaps middle age and after would be more appropriate, when life's *forces* have died into *form*, and the augury for the physical organism is the slow breaking down of that form.

The difference between living words and dead words is well known to the creative writer. The writer confronts at every step the danger that life will be lost in the detail of writing, since the inspiring idea, mood, scene or character can obviously be expressed only through a multiplicity of words. The art of the artist, therefore, consists precisely in striving to animate every detail with the spirit of the whole. It is for this reason that each syllable becomes for any writer a matter of conscience. Words must have just the right movement, tempo, and shaping force—quite beside the right meaning. Writers try to let their subjects choose the necessary form and accent, because they want the life, the soul and the spirit of their subjects to flow without loss into the lines: they want these important realities to show themselves through the magic of words.

What is a matter of conscience for any artist should be felt even more by teachers. The duty to preserve life is for them a sacred obligation, since theirs is the responsibility of seeing to it that real men and women—alive in themselves and tuned to the full reality of existence—are being prepared to take up the world's work.

If we say that the proper task of teachers is to awaken and strengthen the life of thought in their students, it should be obvious that to impart life they must start from life. Hence their duty will not be to transmit bundles of empty fact however well packaged, but to set an example of fully felt, freshly motivated inquiry. To switch metaphors: far less the passive dough of information, far more the vital yeast they can impart to this dough, should be their main concern. In their style is the yeast. The leaven they can add may be trifling in quantity; but if it is a true leaven it will grow. Once the students' thought has been quickened, their achievements will be limited by neither teachers nor texts; for life transcends its first conditions bringing forth higher stages, with new powers, out of itself. What is lacking in programmed instruction is precisely the leavening, quickening element of style.

If, on the other hand, we regard it as teachers' proper task to awaken and strengthen the *will* in the individual students, so that this may flow with the force of single purpose and inexhaustible creativeness, we must again observe that will responds to will. Individuality awakens individuality: the smallest match ignites the largest bonfire. But the words teachers use must issue from the center of their personal realities if they are to touch the core of will in their students. The occasion does not matter, so long as teachers respond to it honestly and with their whole force.

It is fair to ask what presence of mind, what personal force of feeling, what actual will, are to be found in a program conceived far away, at another time, under other conditions, by unknown teachers, and designed for the non-existent "average" student. All this is not of the present, but of the past. Despite admitted small successes, such a concoction does little to arouse the will and much to put the will to sleep. One cannot escape the conclusion that *programs* of any kind in education, whether they be old-fashioned textbooks or new-fashioned computer-assisted, machine operations, obviously work to produce "unreal" people. One trouble is that the further course of the lives of such people will be dangerously easy to control, by social programming.

APPENDIX E, PART 1

Rudolf Steiner on the Experience of Living Thought

The difficulty of grasping the essential nature of thinking by observation lies in this, that it has all too easily eluded the introspecting soul by the time the soul tries to bring it into the focus of attention. Nothing then remains to be inspected but the lifeless abstraction, the corpse of the living thinking. If we look only at this abstraction, we may easily find ourselves compelled to enter into the mysticism of feeling or perhaps the metaphysics of will, which by contrast appear so "full of life." We should then find it strange that anyone should expect to grasp the essence of reality in "mere thoughts." But if we once succeed in really finding life in thinking, we shall know that swimming in mere feelings, or being intuitively aware of the will element, cannot even be compared with the inner wealth and the self-sustaining yet ever moving experience of this life of thinking, let alone be ranked above it. It is owing precisely to this wealth, to this inward abundance of experience, that the counter-image of thinking which presents itself to our ordinary attitude of soul should appear lifeless and abstract.

No other activity of the human soul is so easily misunderstood as thinking. Will and feeling still fill the soul with warmth even when we live through the original event again in retrospect. Thinking all too readily leaves us cold in recollection; it is as if the life of the soul had dried out. Yet this is nothing but the strongly masked shadow of its real nature—warm, luminous and penetrating deeply into the phenomena of the world. This penetration is brought about by a power flowing through the activity of thinking itself—the power of love in its spiritual form.

There are no grounds here for the objection that to discern love in the activity of thinking is to project into thinking a feeling, namely, of love. For in truth this objection is but a confirmation of what we have been saying. If we turn toward thinking in its essence, we find in it both feeling and will, and these in the depths of their reality; if we turn away from thinking towards "mere" feeling and will, we lose from these their true reality. If we are ready to experience thinking intuitively we can also do justice to the experience of feeling and of will; but the mysticism of feeling and the metaphysics of will are not able to do justice to the penetration of reality by intuitive thinking—they conclude all too readily that they themselves are rooted in reality, but that the intuitive thinker, devoid of feeling and a stranger to reality, forms out of "abstract thoughts" a shadowy, chilly picture of the world. (*The Philosophy of Freedom*, p. 119 [This book has also been published as *The Philosophy of Spiritual Activity* and is now published in a new translation as *Intuitive Thinking as a Spiritual Path*]).

APPENDIX E, PART 2

Rudolf Steiner's Concept of Pure Thinking as Spiritual Activity, the Basis and Substance of Freedom

The man who has done more than any other in modern times to restore confidence in the ability of intuitive thought to satisfy the *objective* demands of world reality and the subjective demands of the human soul, is Rudolf Steiner. He found in the spiritual activity of pure thought the basis for human freedom. The following excerpts give some idea of Steiner's affirmation in *The Philosophy of Spiritual Activity*.

This is just the peculiar nature of thinking, that the thinker forgets his or her thinking while actually engaged in it. What occupies one's attention is not one's own thinking, but the object of the thinking, which is being observed.

The first observation we make about thinking is therefore this: that it is the unobserved element in our ordinary mental and spiritual life.

The reason why we do not observe the thinking that goes on in our ordinary life is none other than this, that it is due to our own activity. Whatever I do not myself produce appears in my field of observation as an object; I find myself confronted by it as by something that has come about independently of me. It comes to meet me. I must accept it as something that precedes my thinking process, as a premise. While I am reflecting upon the object, I am occupied with it; my attention is focussed upon it. To be thus occupied is precisely to contemplate by thinking. I attend, not to my activity, but to the object . . . of this activity. In other words, while I am thinking I pay no heed to my thinking, which is of my own making, but only to the object of my thinking, which is not of my making. (pp. 26-27)

There are two things which are incompatible with one another: productive activity and the simultaneous contemplation of it. This is recognized even in Genesis (I, 31). Here God creates the world in the first six days, and only when it is there is any contemplation of it possible: "And God saw everything that he had made and, behold, it was very good." The same applies to our thinking. It must be there first, if we would observe it.

The reason why it is impossible to observe thinking in the actual moment of its occurrence, is the very one which makes it possible for us to know it more immediately and more intimately than any other process in the world. . . . within the whole world content I apprehend myself in my thinking as in that activity which is most uniquely my own. (pp. 27-30)

For everyone, however, who has the ability to observe thinking—and with good will every normal person has this ability—this observation is the most important one he can possibly make. For we observe something of which we ourselves are the creators; we find ourselves confronted, not by an apparently foreign object, but by our own activity. We know how the thing we are observing comes into being. We see into its connections and relationships. A firm point has now been reached from which one can, with some hope of success, seek an explanation of all other phenomena of the world. (p. 29)

When Archimedes had discovered the lever, he thought he could lift the whole cosmos from its hinges, if only he could find a point of support for his instrument. He needed something that was supported by itself and by nothing else. In thinking we have a principle which subsists through itself. (p. 34)

. . . . .

Our thinking is not individual like our sensing and feeling; it is universal. It receives an individual stamp in each separate human being only because it comes to be related to his individual feelings and sensations. By means of these particular colorings of the universal thinking, individuals differentiate themselves from one another. There is only one single concept of "triangle." It is quite immaterial for the content of this concept whether it is grasped in A's consciousness or in B's. It will, however, be grasped by each of the two in their individual ways. (p. 69)

The one uniform concept of "triangle" does not become a multiplicity because it is thought by many persons. For the thinking of the many is in itself a unity. (p. 69)

In thinking we have that element given us which welds our separate individuality into one whole with the cosmos. In so far as we sense and feel (and also perceive), we are simple beings; in so far as we think, we are the all-one being that pervades everything. (p. 70)

One might be tempted to see in the life of feeling an element that is more richly saturated with reality than is the contemplation of the world through thinking. But the reply to this is that the life of feeling, after all, has this richer meaning only for my individual self. (p. 86)

Thinking and feeling correspond to the two-fold nature of our being.... Thinking is the element through which we take part in the universal cosmic process; feeling is that through which we can withdraw ourselves into the narrow confines of our own being.

Our thinking links us to the world; our feeling leads us back into ourselves and thus makes us individuals. Were we merely thinking and perceiving beings, our whole life would flow along in monotonous indifference. Were we able merely to *know* our-selves as selves, we should be totally indifferent to ourselves. It is only because we experience self-feeling with self-knowledge, and pleasure and pain with the perception of objects, that we live as individual beings . . . (p. 86)

Our life is a continual oscillation between living with the univer-sal world process and being our own individual selves. The farther we ascend into the universal nature of thinking, where in the end what is individual interests us only as an example or specimen of the concept, the more the character of the separate being, of the quite definite single personality, becomes lost in us. The farther we descend into the depths of our own life and allow our feelings to resound with our experiences of the outer world, the more we cut ourselves off from universal being. A true individuality will be the one who reaches up with his feelings to the farthest possible extent into the region of the ideal. (p. 87)

. . . . .

Those who find it necessary for the explanation of thinking as such to invoke something else, such as physical brain processes or unconscious spiritual processes lying behind the conscious think-ing which they observe, fail to recognize what an unprejudiced observation of thinking yields. When we observe our thinking, we live during this observation directly within a self-supporting, spiritual web of being. Indeed, we can even say that if we would grasp the essential nature of spirit in the form in which it presents itself most immediately to man, we need only look at the self-sus-taining activity of thinking. (p. 121)

Only if, by means of unprejudiced observation, one has wrestled through to the recognition of this truth of the intuitive essence of thinking will one succeed in clearing the way for an insight into the psycho-physical human organization. One will see that this organization can have no effect on the essential nature of thinking. At first sight this seems to be contradicted by patently obvious facts. For ordinary experience, human thinking makes its appearance only in connection with, and by means of, this organization. This form of its appearance comes so much to the fore that its real significance cannot be grasped until we recognize that in the essence of thinking this organization plays no part whatever. Once we appreciate this, we can no longer fail to notice what a peculiar kind of relationship there is between the human organization and the thinking itself. For this organization contributes nothing to the essential nature of thinking but recedes whenever the activity of thinking makes its appearance; it suspends its own activity, it yields ground; and on the ground thus left empty, the thinking appears. The essence which is active in thinking has a two-fold function: first, it represses the activity of the human organization; secondly it steps into its place. (p. 123)

When we walk over soft ground, our feet leave impressions in the soil. We shall not be tempted to say that these footprints have been formed from below by the forces of the ground. We shall not attribute to these forces any share in the production of the footprints. Just as little, if we observe the essential nature of thinking without prejudice, shall we attribute any share in that nature to the traces in the physical organism which arise through the fact that the thinking prepares its manifestation by means of the body. (p. 123)

An important question, however, emerges here. If the human organization has no part in the essential nature of thinking, what is the significance of this organization within the whole of human nature? Now, what happens in this organization through the thinking has indeed nothing to do with the essence of thinking, but it has a great deal to do with the arising of the ego-consciousness out of this thinking. Thinking, in its own essential nature, certainly contains the real I or ego, but it does not contain the ego consciousness. To see this, we have but to observe thinking with an open mind. The *I* is to be found within the thinking; the *ego-consciousness* arises through the traces which the activity of thinking engraves upon our general consciousness, in the sense explained above. (The ego-consciousness thus arises through the bodily organization. However, this must not be taken to imply that the ego-consciousness, once it has arisen, remains dependent on the bodily organization. Once arisen, it is taken up into thinking and shares henceforth in thinking's spiritual being.) (p. 124)

. . . . .

What is individual in me is not my organism with its instincts and its feelings but rather the unified world of ideas which lights up within this organism. My instincts, urges and passions establish no more than that I belong to the general human species; it is the fact that something of the idea world comes to expression in a particular way within these urges, passions and feelings that establishes my individuality. Through my instincts and cravings, I am the sort of human being of whom there are twelve to the dozen; through the particular form of the idea by means of which I designate myself within the dozen as "I," I am an individual. Only a being other than myself could distinguish me from others by the difference in my animal nature; through my thinking, that is, by actively grasping what expresses itself in my organism as idea, I distinguish myself from others. Therefore one cannot say of the action of a criminal that it proceeds from the idea within that person. Indeed, the characteristic feature of criminal actions is precisely that they spring from the non-ideal human elements. (pp. 137-138)

An action is felt to be free in so far as the reasons for it spring from the ideal part of my individual being; every other part of an action, irrespective of whether it is carried out under the compulsion of nature or under the obligation of a moral standard, is felt to be unfree. (p. 138)

Our life is made up of free and unfree actions. We cannot, however, think out the concept of *human being* completely without coming upon the free spirit as the purest expression of human nature. Indeed, we are human in the true sense only in so far as we are free. This is an ideal, many will say. Doubtless; but it is an ideal which is a real element in us working its way to the surface of our nature. It is no ideal just thought up or dreamed, but one which has life, and which announces itself clearly even in the least perfect form of its existence. (pp. 140-141)

If a human being were merely a natural creature, there would be no such thing as the search for ideals: that is, for ideas which for the moment are not effective but whose realization is required. With the things of the outer world, the idea is determined by the percept; we have done our share when we have recognized the connection between idea and percept. But with the human being it is not so. The sum total of his existence is not fully determined without his own self; his true concept as a moral being (free spirit) is not objectively united from the start with the percept-picture *human being,* needing only to be confined by knowledge afterwards. Human beings must unite *their* concepts with the percept of *human being* by their own activity. Concept and percept coincide in this case only if individuals themselves make them coincide. This they can do only if they have found the concept of the free spirit, that is, if they have found the concept of their own self. (p. 141) [Emphasis added.]

The perceptual object *human being* has in it the possibility of transforming itself, just as the plant seed contains the possibility of becoming a complete plant. The plant transforms itself because of the objective law inherent in it; human beings remain in an incomplete state unless they take hold of the material for transformation within them and transform themselves through their own power. Nature makes human beings merely natural beings; society makes of them law-abiding beings; only we ourselves can make of ourselves free human beings. Nature releases human beings from their fetters at a definite stage in their development, society carries this development a stage further, they alone can give themselves the final polish. The standpoint of free morality, then, does not declare the free spirit to be the only form in which a person can exist. It sees in the free spirit only the last stage of human evolution. (p. 142)

Ethical individualism, then, is the crowning feature of the edifice that Darwin and Haeckel have striven to build for natural science. It is spiritualized theory of evolution carried over into moral life. Anyone who, in a narrow-minded way, restricts the concept of the natural from the outset to an arbitrarily limited sphere may easily conclude that there is no room in it for free individual action. Consistent evolutionists cannot fall prey to such narrow-mindedness. They cannot let the natural course of evolution terminate with the ape, and allow humanity to have a "super-natural" origin; in their very search for the natural progenitors of humanity, they are bound to seek for spirit in nature; again they cannot stop short at the organic functions of human beings, and take only these as natural, but must go on to regard the free moral life as the spiritual continuation of organic life. (pp. 169-170)

Though Maslow was groping after the evolutionary idea Steiner expresses here, what he actually caught hold of as a conception of "spirit in nature" is far different and leads in an opposite direction. The difference between Maslow and Steiner becomes explicit in the following paragraphs. (J.F.G.)

Ethical individualism has nothing to fear from a natural science that understands itself: for observation shows that the perfect form of human action has freedom as its characteristic quality. This freedom must be allowed to the human will in so far as the wills realizes purely ideal intuitions. For these intuitions are not the results of a necessity acting upon them from without, but are due only to themselves. If a person finds that an action is the image of such an ideal intuition, then it is felt to be free. In this characteristic of an action lies its freedom. (pp. 170-171)

It is particularly significant that the right to call an act of will free arises from the experience that an ideal intuition comes to realization in the act of will. This experience can only be the result of an observation, and is so in the sense that we observe our will on a path of development towards the goal where it becomes possible for an act of will to be sustained by purely ideal intuition. This goal can be reached, because in ideal intuition nothing else is at work but its own self-sustaining essence. When such an intuition is present in human consciousness, then it has not been developed out of the processes of the organism but rather the organic activity has withdrawn to make room for the ideal activity. . . . When I observe an act of will that is an image of an intuition, then from this act of will, too, all organically necessary activity has withdrawn. The act of will is free. This freedom of the will cannot be observed by anyone who is unable to see how the free act of will consists in the fact that, firstly through the intuitive element, the activity that is necessary for the human organism is checked and repressed, and then replaced by the spiritual activity of the idea-filled will. Only those who cannot make this observation of the two-fold nature of a free act of will, believe that every act of will is unfree. Those who can make this observation win through to the recognition that man is unfree in so far as he cannot complete the process of suppressing the organic activity; but that this unfreedom tends towards freedom, and that this freedom is by no means an abstract ideal but is a directive force inherent in human nature. People are free to the extent that they are able to realize in their acts of will the same mood of soul that lives in them when they become aware of the forming of purely ideal [spiritual] intuitions. (p. 174)

Steiner's further development of the power of living thought, his spiritual scientific method, can be followed in his *Stages of Higher Knowledge*.

APPENDIX F

Relevant Questions

The following comments were appended to Chapter 6 when it first appeared in 1962 as a *Proceedings* of the Myrin Institute. From different angles, these writers all made the same point I was working on: namely, that psychological, moral, and social conditions call urgently for a renewal of the experience of knowledge.

OWEN BARFIELD

Amid all the menacing signs that surround us in the middle of this twentieth century, perhaps the one which fills thoughtful people with the greatest foreboding is the growing general sense of meaninglessness. It is this which underlies most of the other threats. How is it that the more able man becomes to manipulate the world to his advantage, the less he can perceive any meaning in it? . . .

It remains to be considered whether the future development of scientific man must inevitably continue in the same direction so that he becomes more and more a mere onlooker, measuring with greater and greater precision and manipulating more and more cleverly an earth to which he grows spiritually more and more a stranger. His detachment has enabled him to describe, weigh and measure the processes of nature and to a large extent to control them; but the price he has paid has been the loss of his grasp of any meaning in either nature or himself. . . .

Penetration to the meaning of a thing or process as distinct from the ability to describe it exactly involves a participation by the knower in the known.

"The Rediscovery of Meaning"
(*The Saturday Evening Post*, Jan. 7, 1961)

ARCHIBALD MacLEISH

The real defense of freedom is imagination, that feeling life of the mind which actually knows because it involves itself in its knowing, puts itself in the place where its thought goes.... The man who knows with his heart knows himself to be a man, feels as himself, cannot be silenced. He is free no matter where he lives.... The man who knows with his mind only, who will not commit himself beyond his wits, who will not feel the thing he thinks— that man has no freedom anywhere....

Slavery begins when men give up the human need to know with the whole heart, to know for themselves, to bear the burden for themselves—the "burden," as Wordsworth called it, "of the mystery."

"The Poet and the Press"
(*The Atlantic Monthly*, March, 1959)

RUSSELL W. DAVENPORT

We have said of Western man in general, and of Americans in particular, that they have developed to a very high degree the technique of thinking about things. They have developed very little, and philosophically have neglected almost entirely, the technique of thinking about living entities. The characteristic of thinking about things is that the observer always stays outside of the object of his observation. The characteristic of thinking about living entities is that the observer actually enters into the object in an intuitive way; he lives it, he becomes it; he obtains an understanding of it from the inside, so to speak, where the living truth about it is to be found. It is the thesis of this book that an understanding of this way of thinking is indispensable to the comprehension of freedom.

The Dignity of Man
(New York, Harper & Brothers, 1955, p. 276)

C. S. LEWIS

. . . I think [many modern educators] have honestly misunderstood the pressing educational need of the moment. They see the world around them swayed by emotional propaganda—they have learned from tradition that youth is sentimental—and they conclude that the best thing they can do is to fortify the minds of young people against emotion. My own experience as a teacher tells an opposite tale. For every one pupil who needs to be guarded from weak excess of sensibility there are three who need to be awakened from the slumber of cold vulgarity. The task of the modern educator is not to cut down jungles but to irrigate deserts. The right defense against false sentiments is to inculcate just sentiments. By starving the sensibility of our pupils we only make them easier prey to the propagandist when he comes. For famished nature will be avenged and a hard heart is no infallible protection against a soft head.

The Abolition of Man
(New York, The Macmillan Co., 1947, p. 8)

FRANZ E. WINKLER

The new frontier of our age does not lie in outer space but in the human soul. All the bewildering events of this era are mere portents. They give warning that the torch of individual consciousness can no longer shed sufficient light and meaning on the vast expanse of man's material domain. New resources must be opened in the human soul, if man is not to lose himself in the conquest of outer space or turn his heart to stone while building a civilization of robots.

We are living in a stage of history as much in need of inner exploits as the fifteenth century was of geographical exploration. But the oceans and mountains which must be crossed on this quest are not visible to physical senses and cannot be found on maps and globes. To find them we must restore the sight which began to wane millenniums ago. There is no alternative, for "where there is no vision, the people perish."

Man: The Bridge between Two Worlds
(New York, Harper & Row, 1960, p. 251)

APPENDIX G, PART 1

Education Is Always Religious

(Part of an article by John F. Gardner, reprinted from *Proceedings*, Myrin Institute, 1966)

If it can be demonstrated that education and religion are inseparable, the whole force of the historical battle for freedom of religion will be seen to apply to the battle that must now be fought on behalf of education. Because of the importance I attach to this issue, I have included in its entirety this section of an earlier statement, "Towards a Truly Public Education: A Philosophy of Independence for Schools."

> The essence of education is that it be religious.
> —ALFRED NORTH WHITEHEAD

> From the first, education was the American religion It was— and is—in education that we put our faith; it is our schools and colleges that are the peculiar objects of public largesse and private benefaction; even in architecture we proclaim our devotion, building schools like cathedrals.
>
> . . .
>
> In a personal statement written in 1930, John Dewey said philosophy should "focus about education as the supreme human interest in which, moreover, other problems cosmological, moral, logical, come to a head."
> —HENRY STEELE COMMAGER

> If we have any ground to be religious about anything, we may take education religiously.
> —JOHN DEWEY

Everyone knows that plants turn their leaves and flowers toward the sun, from its rising to its setting. People only seem to be less heliotropic. The sun is the great fact of cosmic weather for humankind. Weather from the cosmos is the background of all our living. Though we may forget it during parts of the day when lesser questions preoccupy us temporarily, we come back to it in many moments. The sun sets the tone of our Earth experience.

What the sun and the sun-filled atmosphere are to our feeling for each day, some conception of divine or ideal being is to our feeling for life as a whole. We can forego the latter as little as the former. No one gladly takes hold of life until they sense that their existence is lighted and warmed by spiritual sunlight. The heart always asks after the inward weather, and the inward weather is always ruled by an ideal sun: that highest value which gives meaning to existence and blesses it to fruitfulness.

This comparison of inner with outer sunlight may help to illustrate what is meant when one maintains that humankind is religious *sui generis*; inveterately and inalienably religious; is religious as the growth of a plant is always heliotropic, or the orbit of a planet is always heliocentric.

People delude themselves with sophistries when they imagine that they have dispensed with the religious experience. As long as they remain human, they will never cease to draw from above and beyond themselves their enthusiasm for living, their power to improve life, their strength and guidance for moral decisions. People may have different theories about the nature of the sun they see, and these differences may lead to fairly important consequences in action; but see the sun they will and must. Dethrone one sun and another rises to take its place, by the force of the whole depth of human nature. Behind all the imperfectly visualized suns shines the primordial sun-power itself. Destroy this objective power for a person, and you destroy that person fundamentally.

"The sun shines into the eyes of an adult, but into the eye and heart of a child," said Emerson. If a grown man needs the sun of the ideal to bring forth his best and deepest, the child is still more dependent. He is more open, more all-one in his devotion.

The child's very existence is trust, hope, and belief. He still sees the world in God. As Wordsworth said, for the child, people and things are still radiant with the invisible light; they yet bear the signature of the divine.

Grownups need to live with religious awareness, aspiration, and discipline, but children need religion still more. If we see this clearly, we are ready to perceive a fundamental truth about the educational institutions in which every modern child's existence is centered from the age of four or five to sixteen or eighteen and beyond. We can perceive that we have been on the wrong track in imagining that a school can ever exclude religion from its teaching. Every school that *satisfies* children is religious. Through curriculum, methods, and attitudes it inevitably cultivates a religious life.

Religious life cannot be successfully developed by the family and church alone, apart from the school. The time to learn how to view the creation as God's handiwork is when created things are being studied for the first time. This occurs in school. Every fact will then speak from its beauty and immediacy the language of God—or none will. And if the school has presented the detail of Nature materialistically, it may be beyond the power of pastor and parents thereafter to bring Deity into a credible relationship with the natural order.

We should not let ourselves be deceived by the belief that public schools are neutral about religion. Neutral they are not. By the necessity of the nature that pulsates and breathes in pupils, teachers, and parents as human beings, every school fosters some form of devotion. The religion that inspires a public school, despite the pose of neutrality, will be one of the traditional faiths, or a zeal for social reform, or some other holy cause.

American public schools are divided chiefly between those which are still rooted in the Protestant Christian impulse that quite consciously and acceptably motivated most of them a century ago, and those which, pressed by changes in the population they serve, have substituted for this religion a new one. The new ideal is generally society-centered; the new faith is called Democracy. It might also be called the American Way of Life. This faith has its hierarchy of power, its credo, its hymn-singing, ceremonies, and ritual. It has been brought forward (always with the close support of Science, a second sacred cause) to satisfy seeking hearts. Citizenship in the democratic society is increasingly represented as the goal of life. Studies need focus, and the preparation for life needs an incentive. These are sought for in the earthly paradise men hope to create.

We have said, then, that education is always religious, in the public school as in a church school. And we have said that the religion which is now coming to the fore with ever-increasing strength in public schools, the sun around which school life is ordered and toward which all eyes are again and again directed with religious feeling, is that of the Great Society, the industrialized-socialized State. That these two characterizations are not without support may be seen in the following quotations from John Dewey.

> Why should we longer suffer from deficiency of religion? We have discovered our lack: let us set the machinery in motion which will supply it. We have mastered the elements of physical wellbeing; we can make light and heat to order, and can command the means of transportation. Let us now put a similar energy, good will, and thoughtfulness into the control of the things of the spiritual life. Having got so far as to search for proper machinery, the next step is easy. Education is the modern universal purveyor, and upon the schools shall rest the responsibility for seeing to it that we recover our threatened religious heritage. (pp. 74-75)

> So far as education is concerned, those who believe in religion as a natural expression of human experience must devote themselves to the development of the ideas of life which lie implicit in our still new science and our still newer democracy. . . . In performing this service, it is their business to do what they can to prevent all public educational agencies from being employed in ways which inevitably impede the recognition of the spiritual import of science and of democracy, and hence of that type of religion which will be the fine flower of the modern spirit's achievement. (p. 86)

If one inquires why the American tradition is so strong against any connection of State and Church why it dreads even the rudiments of religious teaching in state-maintained schools, the immediate and superficial answer is not far to seek. . . . The cause lay largely in the diversity and vitality of the various denominations . . . But there was a deeper and by no means wholly unconscious influence at work. The United States became a nation late enough in the history of the world to profit by the growth of that modern (although Greek) thing—the state consciousness. (p. 78)

Doubtless many of our ancestors would have been somewhat shocked to realize the full logic of their own attitude with respect to the subordination of churches to the state (falsely termed the *separation* of Church and State); but the state idea was inherently of such vitality and constructive force as to carry the practical result, with or without conscious perception of its philosophy. (p. 79)

In such a dim, blind, but effective way the American people is conscious that its schools serve best the cause of religion serving the cause of social unification; and that under certain conditions schools are more religious in substance and in promise without any of the conventional badges and machinery of religious instruction than they could be in cultivating these forms at the expense of a state-consciousness. (pp. 84-85)

—"Religion and Our Schools,"
Education Today

As long as the assumed neutrality of the public schools toward religion masked the situation, one could not see that education is always religious. And one could not go on to draw the inevitable conclusion as regards the proper relation of schools to the state. But the religious nature of public schools is slowly coming at last to be recognized by more and more people who are thoughtful and close to the realities. And the time is coming when we shall have to draw conclusions from our observations.

My own conclusion may be expressed as a syllogism:

A. *The state must be neutral with respect to religious institutions.* The First Amendment to the Constitution of the United States has laid down this true and necessary principle: "Congress shall make no law respecting an establishment of religion. . . ."

B. *In the last analysis schools are religious institutions.* An education that is not at bottom religious is neither serious nor satisfying. On the other hand, a religious attitude toward life that tries to establish itself only through the influence of church and home, leaving the school out of account, will fail, or will create within the mind, heart, and will of children a most painful schism. For the sake of education we need religion, and for the sake of religion we need education: the two are fundamentally inseparable.

C. *Therefore the state must become neutral with respect to the support and control of schools.* Since all serious educational institutions are at the same time religious institutions, the spirit of the First Amendment requires us to realize that the state power should keep hands off the schools as it does off the churches. The state schools must eventually—of course by due process, by many small steps, and, as a matter of harmonious evolution—be disestablished as state churches have been.

The situation that should arise with regard to schools need not by any means be exactly analogous to the present situation of churches in our culture. But, improbable as it may sound to our ears at the moment, the state school as an ideal must be progressively supplanted by the ideal of full independence for all schools.

APPENDIX G, PART 2

Parochial Schools and Freedom of Choice

What will happen to parochial schools, when all schools become schools of choice? Many zealots for the supposedly democratic public school concept fear that were parents really free—that is, economically free—to decide where to send their children for schooling, they would doubtless consign them to a training in sectarian religion or in some other kind of divisive (racial or economic) doctrine. But here again we must visualize the complete picture. When at present parents must choose between religious education that runs the danger of bigotry and the public education that runs the danger of agnosticism and atheism, they will often decide, though not happily, for the former. But when the most varied forms of spiritual impulse can find expression in the schools, who shall say that a predominant percentage of parents will choose any *one* of them?

It is a strange paradox that those who are most fanatical about the necessity for the democratic public school system are also most distrustful of the people. "The people," they fear, "are likely to prefer the tawdry, the fake, the shortsighted, and selfish." But if one does not believe that most people, most of the time, will prefer for their beloved children the best of what is available, on what basis does one's confidence in democracy rest? Our own view is that many people today make such unfortunate choices in their public and private lives because there are so very few really good things to choose from. Just this absence of good choices is the sign of the spiritual poverty of our culture; and this poverty, this spiritual ghetto-condition, has been achieved by several generations of adults educated almost exclusively in state schools.

Dogma and bigotry are not limited to racial, economic, or religious issues. They can be also political. Zeal for democracy can easily mislead. The American way of life is quite rightly equalitarian in political matters, but also quite rightly it is pluralistic in questions of judgment, taste, conviction, and aptitude. We Americans arrive by vote at a single common policy in regard to some issues, but we explicitly forbear to demand, expect, or even wish for unity in regard to others. Just this forbearance from political intrusion is the meaning of our cherished freedom to publish and speak our individual minds, to congregate and collaborate with others of our own persuasion. Does not the Constitution guarantee freedom of conscience and freedom of worship to the individual? Academic freedom, also, has had strong traditional support, however superficially and selfishly we often conceive it nowadays. We do not permit legislation about what shall be considered good art or sound philosophy or scientific truth.

At its best, the American way is pluralistic regarding the substance and much of the process of cultural and spiritual life, but the day must come when we shall realize that the full bearing of the First Amendment should be made still clearer than it is. History should by now have taught us that *whatever is central to the spiritual-cultural striving of humankind* must remain, in Robert MacIver's phrase, "beyond the web of government." The church formerly occupied this central position, but in our time churches have been displaced to a considerable extent by schools. The great question upon which the future of America now depends is not how *church* and state shall be related to one another. That has been settled by the "wall of separation." The great question is: What shall be the relation between *school* and state? The answer to this question should be the same, and for all the same reasons. Far rather than that education be considered a natural function of government, it should be seen as a most unnatural and fundamentally impossible function of government. The wall of separation must be raised between political control and every initiative that properly takes its start from individual judgment and ability, whether this be in science, art, religion, or education.

APPENDIX G, PART 3

Financial Support and Vouchers

Support for the state schools comes presently from various forms of taxation. Support for the independent schools comes from those who can afford to pay double and more for the education of their children. Parochial schools are supported partly by low tuition fees, partly by church subsidies: once again, by citizens who pay double for education, whether they can afford it or not.

How *should* an education that has come of age, that is self-governing, receive support? Since we are not yet at that stage, we had better start from where we are. As education grows more expensive, it is being proposed with ever greater intensity that the principle already recognized for young adults by the G.I. Bill should be extended to cover children of primary and secondary school age as well. Attention is focused on the idea of educational vouchers that will not give governmental support preferentially to any particular kind of school, but will enable parents to give individual support to the school of their own choice.

It may be questioned whether, when we have a wider understanding of the power of truly autonomous education to please and satisfy, and therefore to stimulate the enthusiastic support of all segments of society, the principle of voluntary giving by itself (when school taxes have been eliminated) might raise amounts well beyond what taxes have done. And there is reason to believe that the free gifts of the spirit, as these enter human society through education, should be met by just such human gifts, rising freely from the whole economy like the immeasurably great vapor that rises on a sunny day from the green vegetative world, without in any way exhausting that world. Yet we start just now from taxes, and we are thinking of spending tax money through vouchers; so it is important to be clear about the conditions under which vouchers will prove to be a step forward or a step backward.

The one thing certain is that as far as the principle of freedom is concerned, vouchers may be used either constructively or destructively. If the great majority of citizens continue to be persuaded that state schools are the only right schools, they will cause it to happen that vouchers destroy what remains of educational freedom in America. First the independent and parochial institutions will be invited to become dependent upon support by vouchers; then state or federal regulations will stipulate what must be done by these institutions with their enrollment, curriculum, methods, evaluation procedures, and preparation of teachers, if they are to be deemed worthy of continuing to receive "public monies." Under such conditions, freedom will have been forfeited.

Vouchers could, however, be interpreted in ways that would strengthen educational autonomy, *if* the general public could be brought to realize that freedom is indivisible; that freedom at the university level can never really prosper when freedom at the lower levels is foreclosed; that the school that stands on its own feet will always prove best able to teach the slow learner as well as the fast, the culturally deprived as well as the culturally enriched, the artistically or athletically inclined as well as the student with technical or scientific ambitions; that the responsibility for self-determination in teaching is the only condition capable of attracting the men and women of enterprise and conviction who now steer clear of education; that, with the years, such teachers will grow in vitality and will transform the disappointing schools of today into the cornucopias for creativeness, social idealism, and practical aptitude that the schools of the future can and must become. If and when public opinion inclines to *this* view, voucher arrangements will be interpreted favorably. Unwise restrictions will be avoided. A progressive evolution can then bring us from where we are now to wherever further experience will show that we ought to be.

BIBLIOGRAPHY

Commager, Henry Steele. *Living Ideas in America*. New York: Harper & Brothers, 1951.

Davenport, Russell W. *The Dignity of Man*. New York: Harper & Brothers, 1955.

Dewey, John. *Education Today*. New York: G.P. Putnam's Sons, 1940.

Fromm, Erich. *Man for Himself*. New York: Rinehart and Company, Inc., 1947.

Kelley, Earl and Rasey, Marie. *Education and the Nature of Man*. New York: Harper & Brothers, 1952.

Lewis, C.S. *The Abolition of Man*. New York: The Macmillan Company, 1947.

Maslow, Abraham H. *The Farther Reaches of Human Nature*. New York: The Viking Press, 1971.

—— *Religions, Values, and Peak-Experiences*. New York: The Viking Press, 1964.

—— *Toward a Psychology of Being*. New York: Van Nostrand Reinhold Company, 1968.

Price, Kingsley. *Education and Philosophical Thought*. Boston: Allyn and Bacon, Inc., 1962.

Skinner, B.F. *Beyond Freedom and Dignity*. New York: Alfred A. Knopf, 1971.

—— *Science and Human Behavior*. New York: The Macmillan Company, 1965.

Steiner, Rudolf. *The Child's Changing Consciousness and Waldorf Education*. Anthroposophic Press, Hudson, NY. 1996.

—— *The Education of the Child, And Early Lectures on Education*. Anthroposophic Press, Hudson, NY, 1996.

—— *The Genius of Language: Observations for Teachers*. Hudson, NY: Anthroposophic Press, 1995.

—— *How to Know Higher Worlds: A Modern Path of Initiation.* Hudson, NY: Anthroposophic Press, 1994.

—— *Intuitive Thinking as a Spiritual Path: A Philosophy of Freedom.* Hudson, NY: Anthroposophic Press, 1995.

—— *The Kingdom of Childhood: Introductory Talks on Waldorf Education.* Hudson, NY: Anthroposophic Press, 1995.

—— *The Spirit of the Waldorf School: Lectures Surrounding the Founding of the First Waldorf School, Stuttgart* — 1919. Hudson, NY: Anthroposophic Press, 1995.

—— *Stages of Higher Knowledge.* Spring Valley, New York: The Anthroposophic Press, 1967.

—— *A Theory of Knowledge.* Spring Valley, New York: The Anthroposophic Press, 1968.

—— *The Threefold Social Order.* Spring Valley, New York: The Anthroposophic Press, 1966.

—— *Waldorf Education and Anthroposophy 1: Public Lectures 1921–22.* Anthroposophic Press, Hudson, NY, 1995.

—— *Waldorf Education and Anthroposophy 2: Public Lectures 1923–24.* Anthroposophic Press, Hudson, NY, 1996.

Wann, T.W., ed. *Behaviorism and Phenomenology.* Chicago: University of Chicago Press, 1964.

Winkler, Franz E. *Man: The Bridge between Two Worlds.* Garden City, New York: Waldorf Press, 1975.

. . . .

*For an informative catalog of the work of Rudolf Steiner
and other anthroposophical authors please contact*

ANTHROPOSOPHIC PRESS
RR 4 Box 94 A-1 Hudson, NY 12534
TEL: 518 851 2054
FAX: 518 851 2047